Praise for Lincc

"Richard Carwardine does an exce   the context of nineteenth-century t   that when Lincoln, the man, is romanticized and ennobled, much of the original and authentic richness of his humor and satire is lost. This volume is his attempt to understand Lincoln's use of anecdotes, jokes, and satire in the context in which they occurred. This book both succeeds and deserves a place on any Lincoln collector's bookshelf."

—**Wayne Wolf**, *Civil War News*

"Sorting through the complexities of Lincoln's humor is where Carwardine excels. One of the ways he does this is by showing how Lincoln's sense of humor evolved over time and relative to the case before a jury, the opportunity for political advancement, or the gravity of the nation's existential crisis."   —**Timothy D. Lusch**, *The University Bookman*

"Lincoln's use of jokes and stories is legendary. Not everyone appreciated Lincoln's humor. . . . But Carwardine points out that Lincoln's intrinsic humor was that of a humanitarian and helped contribute to turn his stature as president into statesmanship. There are many other volumes on Lincoln's humor . . . but this is the best succinct version [in] one of the finest volumes in the Concise Lincoln Library of Southern Illinois University Press."

—**Frank J. Williams**, *Civil War Book Review*

"In the years after Lincoln was shot (while enjoying a comic farce), the protectors of his legacy—including those who had so fully appreciated his use of levity during his life—worked to obscure the range and complexity of his humor in the interest of crystalizing the pantheonic Lincoln, the serious-minded savior of the Union. Carwardine has skillfully reilluminated as full a sense of it as can be gleaned short of sharing an afternoon with Lincoln or hearing him on the stump. This is a slim but satisfying study, one that general readers will find enlightening and scholars of the presidency and humor will find most valuable."

—**Peter M. Robinson**, *Journal of Illinois History*

"Far more than a compilation of Lincoln's jokes and stories, this book offers a subtle and sophisticated analysis of the Great Emancipator's richly variegated sense of humor, ranging from almost childish puns and bawdy vulgarity to the cleverest wordplay, withering satire, and hilarious yarns. Especially enlightening is the author's treatment of the solid moral foundation of Lincoln's taste in humorists. This beautifully written study is a worthy companion to Professor Carwardine's prize-winning *Abraham Lincoln: A Life of Purpose and Power.*" —**Michael Burlingame**, editor of *Sixteenth President-in-Waiting: Abraham Lincoln and the Springfield Dispatches of Henry Villard, 1860–1861*

"Ridiculed by political enemies and unappreciated by many allies, Lincoln's sense of humor and bountiful fund of funny stories get a fresh and trenchant analysis in this important study. Richard Carwardine shows how Lincoln's anecdotes not only served a therapeutic function to counter his melancholy but also helped him drive home important points of policy and strategy."
—**James McPherson**, author of *The War That Shaped a Nation: Why the Civil War Still Matters*

"Carwardine interprets Lincoln's propensity for the jocular, especially his use of self-effacing stories, as an essential part of his humanity, a means of dealing with life's ups and downs. Readers will welcome Carwardine's analysis of the richness of Lincoln's frivolity, which adds significance to our understanding of the man, the president, and the legend."
—**John David Smith**, author of *Lincoln and the U.S. Colored Troops*

"This is an important book. Richard Carwardine's study performs the impressive feat of adding new elements and dimensions to our understanding of Lincoln's fabled sense of humor and its significance in his career."
—**Douglas L. Wilson**, author of *Lincoln's Sword: The Presidency and the Power of Words*

"Before you groan ("Not another Lincoln book!"), let me assure you that this compact volume by a leading Lincoln scholar is both illuminating and very funny, containing as it does many instances of our greatest president's humor, in many different registers, from coarse jests to the driest wit."
—**John Wilson**, *Christianity Today*

"Reading this book is a reminder of how gifted historians stitch together the remnants of a lost past to deepen our understanding of the human condition. It is a little gem carved by the hand of a master."

—**Graham Peck**, *Reviews in History*

"In a world where volumes have been written on the subject of each of Lincoln's speeches, all of his limbs, and even his favorite meals, it seems there's also room for a more nuanced exploration of this critical aspect of Lincoln's personality. Luckily, Richard Carwardine is on the case in *Lincoln's Sense of Humor*, a book from the Concise Lincoln Library that I would call necessary, important, and strangely practical. . . .

In the course of anatomizing Lincoln's humor, Carwardine has managed to write a manual essential for anyone intending to use humor in politics. This is guidance a surprising number of people have clamored for. . . . Carwardine could have easily slapped a self-help subtitle on the cover (something like Ageless Lessons in Humorous Communication from the Great Emancipator), added bullet points to the ends of chapters and sold it as a handbook at public speaking and motivation conferences. The world could certainly use an education in what Carwardine identifies as the central root of Lincoln's humor: a moral outrage against hypocrisy and irrational thought and action."

—**Elliott Kalan**, *Journal of the Abraham Lincoln Association*

"Lincoln's exceptional memory and clear fascination with the human experience provided him with a seemingly inexhaustible repertoire of jokes and humorous stories. When paired with his belief in fairness and remarkable ability to pick out a cogent lesson from seemingly any situation, they became his most valuable rhetorical tools. Indeed, one leaves this book suspecting they were also the most appealing part of any encounter with Lincoln. Thus, Richard Carwardine is to be commended for this highly accessible book that adds a new layer to Abraham Lincoln's political genius, while also making him come alive for us just a little bit more."

—**Christian McWhirter**, *American Nineteenth Century History*

CONCISE
LINCOLN
LIBRARY

—

EDITED BY RICHARD W. ETULAIN
AND SYLVIA FRANK RODRIGUE

RICHARD CARWARDINE

Lincoln's Sense of Humor

Southern Illinois University Press
Carbondale

Southern Illinois University Press
www.siupress.com

22 21 20 19   4 3 2 1

The Concise Lincoln Library has been made possible
in part through a generous donation by the Leland E.
and LaRita R. Boren Trust.

Volumes in this series have been published with support from the Abraham Lincoln Bicentennial Foundation, dedicated to perpetuating and expanding Lincoln's vision for America and completing America's
unfinished work.

Jacket illustration adapted from a painting by Wendy
Allen

ISBN 978-0-8093-3777-4

The Library of Congress has catalogued the hardcover
edition as follows:
Names: Carwardine, Richard, author.
Title: Lincoln's sense of humor / Richard Carwardine.
Description: Carbondale : Southern Illinois University
Press, 2017. | Series: Concise Lincoln Library | Includes
bibliographical references and index.
Identifiers: LCCN 2017007441 |
ISBN 9780809336142 (hardback) |
ISBN 9780809336159 (ebook)
Subjects: LCSH: Lincoln, Abraham, 1809–1865—
Humor. | American wit and humor. | BISAC: HISTORY
/ United States / Civil War Period (1850–1877). |
BIOGRAPHY & AUTOBIOGRAPHY / Presidents & Heads
of State. | HUMOR / Topic / Political.
Classification: LCC E457.2 .C355 2017 |
DDC 973.7092—dc23 LC record available at
https://lccn.loc.gov/2017007441

To John Walsh

CONTENTS

LINCOLN'S SENSE OF HUMOR

INTRODUCTION

His flow of humor was a sparkling spring gushing out of a rock—the flashing water had a somber background which made it all the brighter.

—David Ross Locke

There may be no more fitting an introduction to a book on Lincoln's sense of humor than a story at his own expense, one that he thought the best he had ever heard. It involved two Quaker women who, traveling in a railroad car, were discussing the likely outcome of the war.

"I think," one declared, "that Jefferson Davis will succeed."
"And why does thee think so?" asked the other.
"Because Jefferson is a praying man."
"And so is Abraham a praying man."
"Yes; but the Lord will think Abraham is joking!"[1]

The episode highlights several themes central to this study of Lincoln's humor. It delivers a reminder not only of his great relish for the telling of anecdotes and jokes but also of his appetite for repeating them even when—*particularly* when—they were at his own expense: self-mockery was a familiar part of his repertoire. The story equally points to the more or less universal reputation he had acquired over the course of his life as an unsurpassed fount of jocular tales. Yet it shows, too, a conviction among some of his compatriots that this was no proper way for a public figure to behave: how was it possible for ordinary folk to take the nation's commander in earnest if the Almighty himself was unable to do so? Finally, that this much-repeated tale continues to circulate a century and a half after his death reveals how Lincoln's special standing in the pantheon of humorous political leaders continues to inhabit the popular imagination.[2]

Lincoln's contemporaries universally noted his delight in humor; so, too, have his subsequent biographers. In his own time, he was a mold breaker: the first president overtly and consistently to make storytelling and laughter tools of the office. At the Chicago Sanitary Fair in 1864, busts titled *The Two American Humorists* were exhibited: Dan Rice, the blackface minstrel, and Abraham Lincoln. No occupant of the White House has since matched his talent, tactical skill, and openness in this respect, not least because a reputation for too much jocularity has, in more recent times, been deemed politically damaging. Franklin D. Roosevelt's lightheartedness was judged even by his admirers to be undignified; John F. Kennedy, one of the most wry and amusing men to hold the highest office, and who was widely admired as a humorist, still held back in press conferences for fear of appearing unstatesmanlike in the newspaper reports; even Ronald Reagan, who came closest to Lincoln in his skill as a raconteur and readiness to make himself the butt of a joke, was open to the charge that his humor was a substitute for thought and—since he was willing to do "anything for a laugh"—risked becoming "a vaudeville routine."[3] Lincoln by contrast suffered few of the inhibitions felt by later presidents.

In part, this difference was because, as several historians have observed, humor was core to Lincoln's being, a "way of life" and a "habit of mind." It expressed his essential humanity, insofar as humor connotes "an intimate acquaintance with human nature and life, a sense of proportion, and thus of disproportion, a realization of the petty conceits, the affectations, the foibles and weaknesses of men."[4] Those who watched him closely perceived three predominant, separate, but interdependent moods: high-spirited jollity, self-absorbed contemplation, and melancholy. Laughter and sadness were two sides of the same coin. William H. Herndon described his law partner as a "sad-looking man" whose "melancholy dripped from him as he walked."[5] His long-time associate Judge David Davis offered a vivid image: "Mr. Lincoln was not a social man by any means: his Stories—jokes &c. . . were done to whistle off sadness."[6] This was Lincoln's self-diagnosis, too. He told an Iowa congressman that his recourse to humor was an essential relief from his "hours of depression." Using a bow and arrow as a boy, he said, he had learned that "one must let up on the bow if the arrow is to have force." He added, "You flaxen men with broad faces are born with cheer, and don't know a cloud from a star. I am of another temperament.'[7]

The image of Lincoln as a stoic figure—isolated and ground down by the cares of office, personal tragedy, and spiritual crises—is commonplace in both scholarly and popular renderings of the sixteenth president. This perception makes it all the more understandable that his humor and frivolity should be judged an expression of deep psychological need.[8] To read Lincoln's humor in this way, as a reflexive outgrowth of his personality, is beyond reasonable dispute. But this view should not obscure the extent to which Lincoln worked throughout his life to develop the humorist's craft and hone the art of storytelling. As an appreciative reader of Sydney Smith's essays, he would have taken to heart the droll but depressive clergyman's instrumentalist advice on the importance of practical efforts to remedy low spirits: reading amusing books, watching comic drama, and seeking light-hearted company. Lincoln admired resourcefulness; he was as enterprising in his use of humor as he was in political management and leadership. It is true, as James G. Randall stated, that Lincoln's "humor was no mere technique, but a habit of his mind."[9] Yet that technique was an essential and embedded reality, the result of choice and adaptation through practice and experience. The evolution of Lincoln's uses of humor—how he profoundly altered its style and tone to fit the changing needs of his career—merits its own narrative. It forms the subject of chapter 1.

Collections of Lincoln's stories began to appear during his lifetime. They were symptomatic of the boisterous political landscape of mid-nineteenth century America, with its male drinking, singing, gambling, and joke telling.[10] *Old Abe's Joker, or Wit at the White House* (1863), *Old Abe's Jokes, Fresh from Abraham's Bosom* (1864), and *Uncle Abe's Comic Almanac* (1865) were cheap productions that took commercial advantage of the public's appetite for Lincoln's wit, but they mostly repackaged old and hackneyed tales that had never passed his lips. More likely to be authentically Lincolnian were the attributed anecdotes that peppered the wartime newspaper columns and contributed to posthumous compilations.[11] Distinguishing between the genuine and the inauthentic instances of "Lincoln's" humor is as much an art as a science, but Paul M. Zall's recent encyclopedic collections have come closer than any to establishing what are canonical and what are not.[12] What remains surprising is how rarely the sheer richness of Lincoln's humor has been addressed and its complexity analyzed. Contemporaries, even hostile ones, recognized his versatility. "With the caustic wit of Diogenes he combines the best qualities of all the other celebrated jokers of the world," concluded the dyspeptic *New York Herald.* "He is more poetical than Horace, more spicy than Juvenal, more anecdotal than Aesop, more juicy than Boccaccio, more mellow than rollicking Rabelais, and more often quoted than the veteran Joe Miller."[13] Exploring the many-sided character and multiple sources of Lincoln's humor—notably, its western tall tales, morality stories, bawdy jokes, linguistic tricks, absurdities, political satire, and sharp wit—is the purpose of chapter 2.

The third chapter examines one particular dimension of Lincoln's ecumenical taste in humor: his special appetite for satirical work lampooning hypocrisy and ethical double standards. His own satirical compositions enjoyed at best only limited success and in at least one case had troubling consequences. This experience made him all the more appreciative of the razor-sharp satire of a young Ohio newspaperman, David Ross Locke, who shredded the politics and values of the antiadministration Peace Democrats ("Copperheads") through a monstrous creation, the bigoted Petroleum V. Nasby. Lincoln did not use superlatives lightly; when he declared that Locke was a genius for whose satiric gift he would "gladly" relinquish his office, he was making a very special statement. Yet historians have largely ignored the significance of Lincoln's admiration. One explanation for this neglect may be that Nasby's Copperhead theology and the political universe it served are much less accessible to modern readers than they were to Lincoln and his contemporaries. Additionally, there are evident sensitivities in dissecting a text whose intentionally coarse, offensive, and racist language touches a raw nerve in the reader. As one commentator has remarked, in Nasby there is little "softening of vulgarity in deference to public taste."[14] To remedy this neglect, chapter 3 describes Nasby's dubious ethical universe and Locke's purposes in sufficient detail to explain the nuances of Lincoln's pleasure and show the moral springs of his own humor. Certain kinds of levity—satire, above all—can yield insights into the values of those who fashion and appreciate them. Humor in the pursuit of justice has great power. It was Plato who reflected, "Serious things cannot be grasped without ridiculous ones," and it was Aristotle who said, quoting Anacharsis, "Be merry, so you can be serious."[15]

The final chapter addresses the purposes and effects of Lincoln's humor, and illuminates two themes. One is commonly but not systematically addressed in the Lincoln literature: the rich variety of the ends he had in mind with his jokes and stories. His use of humor in speeches and private conversations was rarely for its own sake. Mostly it was designed to secure political or personal advantage, sometimes by frontal assault on opponents, but much more commonly—with both friend and foe—by a mixture of approaches that included lucid exposition through parable, obfuscation through hilarity, refusal through wit, and diversion through cunning. The discussion here aims to provide a more methodical and comprehensive analysis of Lincoln's intent.

The other theme of this chapter—popular reactions to Lincoln's jocularity, particularly the waves of criticism it elicited during his presidency—has largely eluded mainstream scholarly attention. With the passage of time his humor has come to be regarded with a sentimental fondness that was far from universal among his contemporaries. Those who warmed to the wit and wisdom of a storytelling president were matched by others—both radicals and conservatives—who dismissed him as an inadequate, a "Simple Susan," a "smutty joker," and, in Wendell Phillips's derisory words, a "first rate *second rate* man." "President Lincoln is a joke incarnated," sniffed the *New York Herald*, and "has nothing but his jokes to recommend him." These charges were forceful, threatening, and damaging. Some saw him as "a trifling Nero": the "blundering trifler" who jokingly fiddled as the republic burned.[16] The political assault reached its climax during the election of 1864, when the opposition press subverted the popular image of Lincoln the rail-splitter. Now he became the side-splitter and Union-splitter, driving a wedge between North and South.

Lincoln's sense of humor, then, has to be taken seriously. It was an essential element in the thought and practice of both man and president. Appraising its full significance means seeing it within the cultural and political framework of his own time, recognizing its rich variety and complexity of purpose, understanding its ethical dimension, and remaining aware of the political risks that Lincoln ran in "retailing" jokes while the nation—"this republic of suffering"[17]—was engaged in an existential struggle costing at least three-quarters of a million lives. As the nation suffered, so of course did the president. Humor was his lifeline. He found no story more apt than the rueful joke of Justin Butterfield of Chicago, who had been asked at the start of the Mexican-American War whether he opposed it and replied, "no, I opposed one War" (in 1812): "That was enough for me. I am now perpetually in favor of war, pestilence and famine."[18] Such dark levity acted as a tonic, giving Lincoln the strength to pursue more constructive purposes. As the war drew to an end he told a close friend, "die when I may I want it said of me by those who know me best . . . that I always plucked a thistle and planted a flower where I thought a flower would grow."[19] In this strenuous nurturing of the republic, he drew on his strategic wisdom, clarity of principle, skill in political management and communication, grasp of human psychology, and physical and mental strength. This study makes the case that to these ingredients we should add his remarkable and celebrated sense of humor.

THE FACE AND PHASES OF
LINCOLN'S HUMOR

"Lincoln was gifted with an extraordinary sense of humor," recalled a young law student, Gibson William Harris, who worked for a year or so in the Lincoln and Herndon office in Springfield.[1] Although the stern-faced studio photographs of Lincoln, typical of their era, reveal little or nothing of their subject's capacity for laughter, few of those who spent time with him would have challenged Harris's judgment. A face that, at rest, many described as ugly, vulgar, plebeian, and coarse would possess, when animated, what Lincoln's colleague Henry C. Whitney described as "a magnetism and . . . a bonhomie which were indefinable."[2] One associate noted that when transformed by storytelling, winning laughter, and a smile, his face became "a totally different countenance."[3] Robert W. McBride, a member of the president's bodyguard, agreed that "when his face was illumined by a smile all thought of ugliness vanished in its winning and kindly attractiveness."[4] The journalist Horace White declared, "There was more difference between Lincoln dull & Lincoln animated, in facial expressions, than I ever saw in any other human being."[5]

Whether or not his friends and acquaintances shared Lincoln's particular appetite for humor, they all agreed about his distinctive and unrestrained enjoyment of a joke. "Mr. Lincoln's 'laugh' stood by itself," recorded the artist Francis Carpenter. "The 'neigh' of a wild horse on his native prairie is not more undisguised and hearty."[6] Less charitably, George Templeton Strong called it "the laugh of a yahoo, with a wrinkling of the nose that suggests affinity with the tapir and other pachyderms."[7] Gibson Harris described Lincoln's idiosyncratic manner of storytelling: "If he was seated . . . , his feet would be planted flat upon the floor . . . , until near the story's end, at which juncture his eyes would begin to sparkle and his right leg be seen to raise slowly; suddenly, at the instant the climax was reached, the right leg would be thrown across the left, back would go his head, and he would laugh as unrestrainedly as any of his auditors."[8] When Henry Villard, no great admirer, visited Lincoln in Springfield after his election victory in 1860, he noted, "None of his hearers enjoyed the wit . . . of his stories half as much as he did himself. It was a joy indeed to see the effect upon him. A high-pitched laughter lighted up his otherwise melancholy countenance with thorough merriment. His body shook all over with gleeful emotion, and when he felt particularly good over his performances he followed his habit of drawing up his knees, with his arms around them, up to his very face."[9]

Noah Brooks testified to his friend's boundless appetite for colorful tales by recalling an occasion when Lincoln joked at the expense of his secretary of the navy, adding, "I hope Mr. Welles will never hear that I told this story on him." Brooks replied, "It will not be your fault, Mr President, if he does not hear of it, for I have heard you tell it at least a dozen times." Lincoln laughingly conceded the point, saying, "Well, I can't resist telling a good story."[10] He acknowledged his lifelong appetite for jokes and humorous tales: intrinsic to his well-being, they were regular features of his private conversations and informal exchanges. The public expression of his sense of humor, however, varied over time. At key moments, first in the 1840s and again, more emphatically, in the 1850s, he reined in an earlier impulse for sarcasm, comic hurt, and satirical assault. In part this restraint was the effect of growing maturity: his personal transformation, as he advanced into his prime, naturally reinforced the discipline with which he exercised his humor. But it was also shaped, over the course of his career, by what he calculated would best serve his advancement, and—as president—would help him in steering the nation through its greatest crisis.

Young Abraham

Several of the characteristic features of the adult Lincoln's distinctive sense of humor were already apparent during his early years. The boy who wrote in his arithmetic notebook

> Abraham Lincoln
> his hand and pen
> he will be good but
> god knows When

and

> Abraham Lincoln is my nam[e]
> And with my pen I wrote the same
> I wrote in both hast and speed
> and left it here for fools to read

was already drawn to the wry humor that would nestle in memorable passages of his later writing.[11] His appetite and aptitude for public speaking surfaced at about the age of ten when, standing on a log or tree stump, he would entertain a gathering of other children. His keen ear for language and tone allowed him to repeat almost word for word the sermons of the Baptist preachers he heard in church services. Tilda Johnston, his stepsister, recalled that "Abe would take down the bible, read a verse—give out a hymn—and we would sing . . . he would preach & we would do the Crying—sometimes he would join in the Chorus of Tears"; he gave free rein to his love of the ridiculous, once praying that God would put stockings on the feet of chickens in winter.[12] His irreverent mimicry of impromptu preaching and prayer, and religious enthusiasm, "did Especially tickle the Children" but earned his father's stern reproof. His stepmother, Sarah, agreed that "Abe was always fond of fun—sport—wit & jokes," while Dennis Hanks, his cousin, described him as "a cheerful boy—a witty boy—was humorous always—sometimes would get sad—not very often—He would Joke—tell stories—run rigs [tease and pour ridicule]—&c on the boys."[13] The pranks he played as a child heralded the fond indulgence with which later, as a father, he would treat the exuberant misbehavior of his own boys.

During his Indiana years Lincoln revealed another facet of his humor: an appetite for cruel personal ridicule. William H. Herndon recorded how the teenager used a sharp satirical pen "to lampoon those who provoked in any way his especial displeasure." The most notorious of these youthful pieces—"The First Chronicles of Reuben"—comprised a score-settling assault on the leading family in his neighborhood, the Grigsbys. Lincoln's sister Sarah had married Aaron Grigsby in 1826 but died in childbirth less than two years later. What precisely lay behind Lincoln's estrangement from the family is unclear, but he took the occasion of the joint wedding of two Grigsby brothers—Reuben and Charles—to circulate a satirical account of their wedding night. Using a scriptural idiom, Lincoln tells a farcical tale of brides put to bed with the wrong grooms: "It came to pass," he wrote, that the mother "ran to one of the beds and exclaimed, 'O Lord, Reuben, you are in bed with the wrong wife.'" The episode itself was not a complete fiction, for Lincoln had used complicit insiders to swap the beds and secure the nocturnal confusion, but it was his anonymous satire that really stung the family—and he compounded their embarrassment by quickly following it up with verses ridiculing another Grigsby brother, William:

> . . . Reuben and Charles have married two girls,
> But Billy has married a boy.
> The girls he had tried on every side,
> But none could he get to agree;
> All was in vain, he went home again,
> And since then has married to Natty.
> So Billy and Natty agreed very well,
> And mamma's well pleased with the match.
> The egg it is laid, but Natty's afraid
> The shell is so soft it never will hatch,
> But Betsy, she said, 'You cursed bald head,
> My suitor you never can be,
> Besides your low crotch proclaims you a botch,
> And that never can answer for me.

In Herndon's words, "These crude rhymes and awkward imitations of scriptural lore demonstrated that their author if assailed, was merciless in satire." The episode showed Lincoln the political possibilities of public ridicule and the power it conferred on those who wielded it. What he called "the power to hurt" would remain a telling, though not the chief, weapon in his rhetorical armory.[14]

Leaving home for good in 1831, and turning his back on the drudgery of farm labor, Lincoln carried with him high intelligence, a genial manner, and an astonishing natural gift: a memory that could effortlessly produce an apt story from the ever-accumulating file of anecdotes and jokes stored in his well-stocked mind. In the various employments and enterprises at which he tried his hand over the next six years—river man, storekeeper, army captain, postmaster, surveyor, lawyer, and legislator—Lincoln's bonhomie and capacity to entertain served him as well as any of his other considerable qualities, and aided his advancement.

During the few weeks Lincoln spent at the small settlement of Sangamo Town in 1831, building the flatboat for the goods that Denton Offutt had hired him to transport to New Orleans, his skill and practical ingenuity won many admirers. So, too, did his prowess in storytelling. Residents were struck by the contrast between the newcomer's striking physical appearance ("long—tall & green") and ill-fitting clothes ("trowsers short—not Strapt down . . . broad brim low wool hat"), and his intelligent, compelling conversation. During the noon break and again in the evening men would gather near the sawmill, lounging on a long log stripped of its bark, swapping yarns and whittling wood. They quickly discovered that their company included an irresistibly droll raconteur. According to John Roll, as soon as Lincoln delivered the punch line of a story, "the boys on the log would whoop and roll off," eventually giving the seat a high polish. They called it "Abe's log"—a name that lingered, together with his tales, long after he had left the place. Caleb Carman, a Democrat bitterly opposed to Lincoln's politics, still "loved the Man" for being "allways very mery & full of fun," and able to take a joke at his own expense.[15]

Lincoln came to be similarly appreciated in the aspiring village of New Salem, where he lived from 1831 to 1837. Starting out as a clerk in Offutt's store, he was—in the words of another resident, Royal Clary—"humorous—witty & good natured & that geniality drew him to our notice So quick." Jason Duncan, who arrived in the summer of 1831 to practice medicine, warmed to Lincoln's "open frank manner" which, "coupled with a flow of good humor and great witticism, always made him a welcome member of any group or Society of intellegent men."[16] Theodore Gains Onstot recalled Lincoln's great power of mimicry and unequaled storytelling. "He could perfectly mimic a Dutchman, Irishman or Negro"; men "laughed at his stories until they had almost shaken their ribs loose"; long-standing sufferers from physical ills would listen to Lincoln "and laughed their ailments away."[17]

As captain of a New Salem company in the Black Hawk War— elected for his popularity and not his frankly negligible military qualities—Lincoln kept his men's respect as a leader because, according to Major John T. Stuart, "he was a good clever fellow"; admired as a strong wrestler, he was also esteemed "for being a kind genial and companionable man, a great lover of jokes and teller of stories." Stuart maintained, "Everybody liked him—he told good anecdotes and was always very entertaining and amusing—he became very popular in the army."[18] During the short military campaign, William Miller recalled, the hard days were lightened during the evenings by racing, jumping, and telling anecdotes, "in which Lincoln Beat all Keeping up a constant Laughter and good humor among the soldiers."[19] Thanks to his "cheerfulness . . . buoyancy & elasticity," the "whole company, even amid trouble and suffering, received Strength & fortitude."[20] William G. Greene, another volunteer, reported that in consequence Lincoln "was idolized by his men."[21]

On his return to New Salem, Lincoln—now working in Offutt's store—began to contemplate a career in politics, and in his leisure hours studied both law and surveying. One young resident recalled, "He Commenced reading law in 1832 & 3—read in the mornings & Evenings—would play at vari[ou]s games—jumping—running— hopping telling stories & cracking jokes."[22] His law texts included books that his mentor, Judge Bowling Green, had lent him; he occasionally practiced in the judge's court. Green found Lincoln "both amuseing and instructive, so laconic often as to produce a spasmodic shaking of the verry fat sides of the old law functionary."[23] Lincoln's talent, which secured his formal enrollment as a lawyer in 1837, was both comic and forensic. As a surveyor, too, Lincoln commanded his neighbors' attention by his reputation for humor. When "he got a job there was a picknick and jolly time in the neighborhood. Men and boys would gather around ready to carry chains, drive stakes and blaze trees—but mainly to hear Lincoln's odd stories and funny jokes—interspersed with foot races and wrestling matches in which Lincoln was always the victor, when persuaded to take a hand."[24]

Equally, Lincoln's political aspirations benefited from the genial good humor that accompanied his practical capabilities and high intelligence. His first run for the state legislature, in 1832, resulted in electoral defeat but—hearteningly—secured him the overwhelming support of the New Salem precinct. Lincoln's belief in the village's future well-being—and of the state as a whole—mirrored his faith in the economic program laid out by Henry Clay and the nascent Whig party. Although New Salem's 300 voters were mostly Democrats, Lincoln received 277 of the community's ballots. This, clearly, was a personal vote. Admired as "an honest and worthy young man," Lincoln was also a winning, likable presence whose wit and sense of fun made him a magnet in any company.[25]

These were the personal qualities that served Lincoln admirably in his pursuit of political office, as he strove to become more widely known. Years later, John G. Nicolay identified key elements in the successive election victories that, from 1834, gave Lincoln four terms in the Illinois legislature: his language and levity. Speaking to "plain people"—whether soliciting their votes in their cabins or surveying their farm lines—he avoided rhetorical extravagance and high-sounding words, instead drawing on "the simple modes of thought and strong rural phraseology he had learned as a boy." Large gatherings of settlers were hard to come by, so whenever there was a neighborhood occasion—a shooting match, for example, or a cabin raising—a candidate for office would seize his chance to speak. Especially propitious were evening meetings in candle-lit schoolhouses. "Here the speaker needed all his epigrams and anecdotes to dissipate . . . the staring solemnity, of his auditors in the ghostly half-light inside and the dismal darkness and loneliness outside the little cabin. These talks were uncongenial soil for rhetoric and literary style. They needed to be seasoned with pithy argument and witty illustration, and rendered in a vocabulary that had the flavor of the cabin and the energy of the frontier." Lincoln, the plainspoken and humorous storyteller, was in his element.[26]

At the same time, Lincoln's "power to hurt" offered a resource that, when deployed with satirical edge, could have withering effect. Such was memorably the case during Lincoln's campaign for reelection to the state legislature in 1836, when he spoke before a large crowd in Springfield. His close friend Joshua F. Speed vividly recalled the occasion. Lincoln's "very able" speech prompted a request from George Forquer—a prominent local lawyer and Democrat—that he be given the stand. A recent convert from the Whig party, Forquer had been rewarded by his new associates with a lucrative public office; he had also built the best house in the city, over which he had erected a lightning rod, "the only one in the place." Fifteen years Lincoln's senior, the patronizing Forquer declared "that the young man would have to be taken down" and, oozing superiority, set about his task. After waiting with "suppressed excitement," Lincoln resumed the stand. He acknowledged he was young, but his critic should remember, "I am older in years than I am in the tricks and trades of politicians. I desire to live, and I desire place and distinction; but I would rather die now than, like the gentleman, live to see the day that I would change my politics for an office worth three thousand dollars a year, and then feel compelled to erect a lightning rod to protect a guilty conscience from an offended God." Speed did not say how far, if at all, his eviscerating assault was delivered with jocularity or lightness of tone.[27] Whatever the mode, the rhetoric itself was powerfully inflected with righteous indignation and ridicule. In another speech during that campaign Lincoln took on the Democrats' chief spokesman, Jacob Early, and "riddled the man" with ridicule.[28] As he matured, Lincoln had no habitual recourse to such excoriating wit, but his speed of thought and capacity for a well-turned phrase would remain key weapons in his armory.

Springfield and Washington, D.C., 1837–50

When in 1837 Lincoln moved from New Salem to Springfield, the short journey marked a huge stride in his professional and social advancement. Nearing his thirtieth year, he joined the law practice of John T. Stuart, as a junior partner. At the same time, as one of the leading Whigs in the Illinois Assembly, his political mastery came to be admired—and deployed—well beyond the limits of the state capital. In Mary Todd, his wife-to-be, he encountered a young woman with a kindred sense of humor: according to her sister, "she occasionally indulged in sarcastic, witty remarks, that cut like a damascus blade, but there was no malice behind them. She was full of humor, but never unrefined."[29] Marriage, fatherhood, a legal partnership with William H. Herndon, and a term in the U.S. House of Representatives were the landmark features of the next decade. By 1850 he was an instantly recognizable and admired citizen of Springfield, prospering professionally and materially in a world far removed from his rustic roots. Yet his tastes and habits remained quite simple. He never became so acculturated to his bourgeois environment that he lost touch with the experience of plain folk. One measure of this continuity was his persisting recourse to the humor and stories of the rural society he had left but to which he remained connected by his travels on political and legal business. Equally significant, however, was the way in which the maturing Lincoln would come to discipline his humor just as he exercised self-control as a husband, father, and successful lawyer. Learning to bridle his use of sarcasm and satire was part of a larger personal transformation.

In private or social settings during these years, little changed in the way Lincoln shared the enjoyment of his humorous tales. Isaac N. Arnold, a fellow lawyer, described the hospitality that he and Mary offered friends and companions during the terms of the court and sessions of the legislature. Their genial manner and Lincoln's "wit and humor, anecdote, and unrivalled conversation . . . formed the chief attraction, and made a dinner at Lincoln's cottage an event to be remembered."[30] In the exclusively masculine environment of the Lincoln and Herndon law office, the conversational exchanges prompted more uninhibited enjoyment. Gibson Harris could barely believe his good luck: "I wish you co[uld] be in the office about two hours, to hear Lincoln tell his tales and anecdotes, of which he has any amount," the young student wrote to a friend. "I think you would laugh yourself well in that length of time. I [am] sometimes . . . so convulsed with laughter as to be almost unable to keep my seat. I have seen a dozen or more, with their hands on their sides[,] their heads thrown back, their mouths open, and the tears coursing down their cheeks, laughing as if they would die, at some of Lincoln's jokes."[31] On occasion, Lincoln would take local boys fishing on the Sangamon. These were daylong treats, punctuated by a riverbank picnic lunch. "Mr. Lincoln sat down with us," one of the youngsters recalled. "When we had eaten he told us stories and entertained us with his funny comments. No boy . . . on one of these fishing trips willingly missed another."[32]

Lincoln's personal ambition and self-confidence led him to indulge in a more reckless form of humor: assaulting political opponents through both public ridicule and the semicloaked attack of anonymous or pseudonymous satire. Two experiences in particular would teach him the painful lesson that undisciplined and self-indulgent humor could injure its author as well as its intended target. One occurred during Lincoln's campaign for the legislature in 1840, when he responded to a stinging speech of Judge Jesse B. Thomas with an even more withering reply. It was the manner not the matter of Lincoln's riposte that caused the sensation: "for the first time, on the stump or in public," Herndon recorded, he "resorted to mimicry for effect." To the yells and cheers of the crowd, Lincoln—an unrivaled mimic—imitated the judge's peculiarities of gesture and voice, "caricaturing his walk and the very motion of his body." This scathing ridicule was too much for the victim, who broke down and "began to blubber like a baby." The "skinning" of Thomas, as the event came to be known, was "so unlike Lincoln" that it was recalled years afterward. Lincoln himself confessed to Herndon that he had gone too far and the memory "filled him with the deepest chagrin." He sought out Thomas and made a generous apology. He had won the debate—but at quite a cost.[33]

The second episode occurred two years later. Its roots lay in the empowerment Lincoln experienced with the "Chronicles of Reuben" and later with several satirical contributions to the *Sangamo Journal*.[34] A cluster of unattributed articles during the summer of 1837 aimed to help his friend Anson G. Henry win election as probate justice of the peace. Lincoln was convinced that James Adams, the pompous incumbent, had forged documents to secure for himself the land of a deceased client. Writing as "Sampson's Ghost," Lincoln charged Adams with fraud and fashioned a lampoon ("A Ghost! A Ghost!"), in which the drunken forger was confronted by the anguished specter of his victim. Shortly before the election yet another story, in all likelihood also Lincoln's handiwork, ridiculed the bulky Adams:

> The recent noise and excitement made about the wounds and bruises received by Gen. Adams, reminds me of an adventure . . . many years ago. Not far from this place I met a sucker late in the evening returning to his home. "Good evening friend," said I. "How far is it to Springfield?" "Well, I guess its about five miles." . . . "What's the news there?" "Well, there's nothing of any account but a sad accident that happened the other day:—you don't know Gineral Adams?—Well, the Gineral went to stoop down to pick some blackberries and John Taylor's calf gave him a butt right—" "You don't say so,—and did the Gineral die?" "No, by G . . . , but the calf did!"[35]

Lincoln produced further pieces of anonymous satire in 1841, one of them ridiculing Stephen A. Douglas for opposing "life offices" while at the same time accepting one as a supreme court judge.[36]

Lincoln's taste for ridicule through satire would, however, soon lose its relish, the result of a painful episode in September 1842. The occasion was Lincoln's witty pseudonymous assault on the state auditor, thirty-six-year-old James Shields, whose office had announced that tax collectors would cease to accept the discounted notes issued by the state bank. In a semiliterate letter "from the Lost Townships," written in dialect and signed "Rebecca," Lincoln used the platform of the *Sangamo Journal* to play with outraged wry humor on the Democrats' argument that to accept paper money would expose the state to a "danger of loss." Then "aunt Becca" widened her disdain to ridicule Shields himself, calling him "a fool as well as a liar" for whom "truth is out of the question, and as for getting a good bright passable lie out of him, you might as well try to strike fire from a cake of tallow." Known for his vanity and self-regard, Shields was an easy and inviting target: Lincoln could not resist a thrust at this "conceity dunce":

> I seed him when I was down in Springfield last winter. They had a sort of a gatherin there one night, among the grandees, they called a fair. All the galls about town was there, and all the handsome widows, and married women, finickin about, trying to look like galls, tied as tight in the middle, and puffed out at both ends like bundles of fodder that hadn't been stacked yet, but wanted stackin pretty bad. . . . I looked in at the window, and there was this same fellow Shields floatin about on the air, without heft or earthly substance, just like a lock of cat-fur where cats had been fightin.
>
> He was paying his money to this one and that one, and tother one, and sufferin great loss because it wasn't silver instead of State paper; and the sweet distress he seemed to be in,—his very features, in the exstatic agony of his soul, spoke audibly and distinctly—"Dear girls, *it is distressing,* but I cannot marry you all. Too well I know how much you suffer; but do, *do* remember, it is not my fault that I am *so* handsome and *so* interesting."
>
> As this last was expressed by a most exquisite contortion of his face, he seized hold of one of their hands and squeezed, and held on to it about a quarter of an hour.[37]

Shields, an impetuous man on a short fuse, had good reason to rage at the insult—with its sexual insinuations and demeaning assault on his character—and to smart at the sharp teasing it prompted on the streets of Springfield. He insisted that the *Journal*'s editor identify the author. Consenting, Lincoln received Shields's demand for "a full, positive and absolute retraction" and an apology for the degrading personal insults he had suffered.[38] Unconvinced that he had overstepped the reasonable boundaries of political satire and unwilling to yield to a menacing demand, Lincoln refused. Conscious that the whole town was watching, Shields challenged him to a duel. Lincoln accepted, despite his principled antipathy to dueling, but soon regretted appointing as his second Dr. Elias H. Merryman, who showed little appetite for a negotiated outcome. Telling Albert T. Bledsoe, "I don't care about fighting just to gratify Dr. Merry-man," Lincoln followed his Whig colleague's advice over weapons, which were Lincoln's to choose.[39] Bledsoe believed Shields had more bluster than bravery and would back out if Lincoln elected to use broadswords, not the customary pistols or rifles. Eight inches taller than Shields, he would have a huge advantage in reach.

We cannot be sure how far Lincoln intended the dark humor that lurked in his selection of weapons—"Cavalry broadswords of the largest size, precisely equal in all respects"—and the layout of the dueling area: two rectangular spaces, one for each combatant, separated by a ten-foot-long plank set on its edge, to be crossed by neither party.[40] Certainly, the choice of barbarous weaponry and disdain for the spirit of the honor code were rich in irony, and doubtless intended as such. But Lincoln was probably too preoccupied to reflect much on the grim humor of the whole business: he was busy learning how to handle both the broadsword and the embarrassment—shame, even—that he felt for allowing himself to be entangled in this imbroglio. He did, however, manage a joke on his way to the dueling ground, past the hundreds who had turned out to watch. He was reminded, he said, of the young Kentuckian whose sweetheart, as he was leaving home to fight in 1812, presented him with a belt embroidered with the motto, "Victory or Death." "Isn't that rather too strong?" the grateful volunteer said. "Suppose you put 'Victory or Be Crippled.'"

When the two parties finally met, swords in hand on Bloody Island (Missouri), the seconds managed to avert the duel. Lincoln, much relieved, never succeeded in wholly suppressing the shame he felt over the affair. The episode did him no favors among his fellow Whigs: he was sure that he failed to win the party's congressional nomination in 1843 "because I had talked about fighting a duel."[41] It continued to dog him politically into the 1850s and was a subject he always sought to deflect. He and Mary agreed not to allude to what had happened and—even worse—what was narrowly averted. Never again would Lincoln write insulting anonymous or pseudonymous satire. He recognized that, taken to extreme, ridicule could damage its author as well as its victim. If, as is quite likely, Lincoln found the phrase "the power to hurt" in Shakespeare's sonnet 94, he would have had to confront the poet's praise of those "who have pow'r to hurt and will do none."[42] This superior sentiment was of a piece with his embrace of a more manly and self-disciplined mode of political opposition, one that chimed with broader contemporary redefinitions of northern masculinity. Although he continued to lampoon his political opponents, he now did so openly, and would never come even close to risking an outcome as shocking as his near-duel with James Shields.

Satirical self-censorship was no great sacrifice for a politician, lawyer, and neighbor with a rich variety of other means of inducing laughter. In the legislature, the courtroom, and the tavern Lincoln easily won people over with his sense of humor and genial, likable manner. Though awkward in appearance and speaking with an unusually reedy voice, he won attention by his uncomplicated language, lucid exposition, and genuine wit. Even his opponents recognized that Lincoln's command of an audience had to do with his ability to make them laugh while he engaged seriously with his opponent's argument. Campaigning in the presidential canvass of 1840, he impressed Democrats with his calm assurance and geniality in the cut-and-thrust of public debate. A reporter from that party's heartland of southern Illinois noted "he seldom loses his temper, and always replies jocosely and in good humor"; consequently "the evident marks of disapprobation which greet many of his assertions, do not discompose him, and he is therefore hard to foil."[43]

As he reined in his satirical gusto, Lincoln avoided the cruel humor of wounding personal assault, but he continued to deploy pertinent jokes at the expense of his political foes. He had refined his ability to deflate an opponent with a well-timed country tale. During a debate in the legislature to introduce a tax increase and bond issue to complete the ambitious Illinois and Michigan Canal project, he was ridiculed by a Democrat from Montgomery who likened his appetite for debt to an Arkansas drunkard stupefied after taking too much of "the *cretur*." The insensible man resisted all attempts to revive him until, hearing a neighbor recommend some "brandy toddy," he rose and said "that is the stuff": so it was with Lincoln's dependency on debt. Lincoln shot back at once, by likening his opponent to an eccentric old Indiana bachelor who "was very famous for seeing *big bugaboos* in every thing." One day, while out hunting, the man began "loading and firing as fast as possible in[to] the top of a tree." His brother came to investigate and, seeing nothing, asked him what he was firing at. "A squirrel," the bachelor replied, continuing to fire. "His brother believing that there was some humbug about the matter, examined his person, and found on one of his eye lashes a *big louse* crawling about. It is so with the gentleman from Montgomery. He imagined he could see squirrels every day, when they were nothing but *lice*."[44] The speed and aptness of Lincoln's reply "convulsed the whole house." Members of both parties laughed, "screamed and yelled," "thumped upon the floor with their canes," "clapped their hands," "threw up their hats," "shouted and twisted themselves into all sorts of contortions, until their sides ached and the tears rolled down their cheeks."[45]

During the presidential campaign of 1848 Lincoln reserved his particular scorn for the Democrats' nominee, Lewis Cass. Speaking on the floor of the House, occasionally stopping at his desk to consult a few pages of notes, he strode up and down the aisle, "holding his left hand behind him so that he could now and then shake the tails of his own rusty, black broadcloth dress-coat, while he earnestly gesticulated with his long right arm, shaking the bony index finger at the Democrats on the other side of the chamber."[46] He challenged "the Great Michigander" over matters of policy—above all Cass's equivocation over internal improvements and the Wilmot Proviso, which aimed to halt slavery's westward advance—and, to great mirth in the chamber and his own evident relish, he poked fun at the senator's record in public service. Jeering at the legion of campaign biographers who tried to cloak Cass in the martial garb of Andrew Jackson ("tying him to a military tail, like so many mischievous boys tying a dog to a bladder of beans"), Lincoln dismissed the candidate's record in Canada during the war of 1812 as at best negligible. With heavy irony, he likened Cass's experience to his own role as "a military hero" during the Black Hawk war: "I fought, bled, and came away. . . . I bent a musket pretty badly on one occasion . . . by accident. . . . [I saw no] live, fighting Indians . . . but I had a good many bloody struggles with the musquetoes." Cass might be able to claim a superior record in picking whortleberries, during the battle of the Thames, but "I guess I surpassed him in charges upon the wild onions."[47]

Speaking of charges, Lincoln punningly continued, Cass's most successful ones had been upon the public treasury. During his seventeen years as governor of Michigan Territory, Cass had claimed and received more than $96,000. "This large sum was reached, by assuming that he was doing service, and incurring expenses, at several different *places,* and in several different *capacities* in the *same* place, all at the same *time.*" Cass was a large man, whom Lincoln had earlier called with irony "comparatively small," when measured against Andrew Jackson. Now he played upon his size and appetite:

> at eating too, his capacities are shown to be quite . . . wonderful. From October 1821 to May 1822, he ate ten rations a day in Michigan, ten rations a day here in Washington, and near five dollars worth a day besides, partly on the road between the two places! . . . Mr. Speaker, we have all heard of the animal standing in doubt between two stacks of hay, and starving to death. The like of that would never happen to Gen: Cass; place the stacks a thousand miles apart, he would stand stock still midway between them, and eat them both at once; and the green grass along the line would be apt to suffer some too at the same time. By all means, make him President, gentlemen. He will feed you bounteously,—if—if there is any left after he shall have helped himself.[48]

Lincoln's speech drew plaudits from members of both parties. Its vigor in argument, irony, and wit led older members to liken his rhetorical skill to the debating panache of Tom Corwin of Ohio—the ultimate accolade for any congressman using laughter as an effective weapon. Invigorated, Lincoln carried this blend of serious intellectual rigor and comic leavening onto the campaign trail in New England in support of his party's candidate, Zachary Taylor. In the handsome City Hall at Worcester, the Whig faithful of Massachusetts heard him for the first time. One of them, Henry J. Gardner, described the inauspicious initial impression Lincoln made: "his tall, angular, bent form, and his manifest awkwardness and low tone of voice, promised nothing interesting." As he warmed up, however, and the audience adjusted to his quaint, western style of speaking, the mood changed. "He . . . told stories admirable in humor and in point, interspersed with bursts of true eloquence, which constantly brought down the house. His sarcasm at the expense of Cass, Van Buren and the Democratic party was inimitable, and whenever he attempted to stop, the shouts of 'Go on! go on!' were deafening." Deploying his driest humor, he gave offense when he said, "I have heard you have abolitionists here. We have a few in Illinois and"—referring to the murder of Elijah P. Lovejoy in 1837—"we shot one the other day." In the most intensely antislavery state in the Union, the remark was ill-judged: criticized in the Free Soil press, he did not repeat it. What lingered positively in the public mind, however, was his jibe at the platform of the newly formed Free Soil party, which, he declared, offered no principle except opposition to slavery's extension: if it "held any other, it was in such a general way that it was like the pair of pantaloons the Yankee pedler offered for sale, 'large enough for any man, small enough for any boy.'"[49] Lincoln's success in Worcester and several other venues impressed fellow Whigs with what a Bostonian praised as "sound reasoning, cogent argument and keen satire" of a sort rarely equaled.[50]

During his term as congressman, Lincoln carried his distinctive fondness for storytelling into his casual social encounters in Washington, whether with players at the bowling alley, or newspapermen, or fellow raconteurs in the post office at the Capitol, or, above all, his fellow residents at Mrs. Sprigg's boardinghouse. James Pollock, a Whig representative from Pennsylvania, found Lincoln "a genial & pleasant companion—full of good humor, ready wit and with an unlimited fund of anecdote, which he would relate with a zest and manner that never failed to bring down the 'Mess,' and restore harmony & smiles, when the peace of our little community was threatened by a too earnest or heated controversy."[51] A young medical student, Samuel C. Busey, was equally impressed with Lincoln's conciliatory use of "amusing jokes, anecdotes, and witticisms" as a conversational balm. When Lincoln was "about to tell an anecdote during a meal," he would "lay down his knife and fork, place his elbows upon the table, rest his face between his hands, and begin with the words 'that reminds me,' and proceed. Everybody prepared for the explosions sure to follow."[52] When, on occasion, Lincoln took a leisurely Saturday breakfast with Daniel Webster, his humorous reflections on events, "sparkling with spontaneous and unpremeditated wit," delighted his host and other "solid men of Boston." With his "endless *répertoire* of [stories] always ready, like the successive charges in a magazine gun, and always pertinently adapted to some passing event . . . this bright specimen of western genius" came to be known, said Ben Perley Poore, "as the champion story-teller of the Capitol."[53]

Springfield, 1850–61

Returning to Springfield on the completion of his single congressional term, Lincoln had mixed feelings about his time in Washington. Henry C. Whitney thought that in the House he had "attempted grave political philosophy and the witchery of broad humor, each alike in vain; and . . . returned home with neither profit nor laurels."[54] Whether or not Lincoln's own verdict was quite so bleak, he had no appetite to return to Congress: it was to the law and not politics that he directed most of his professional attention over the next four or five years.

As a circuit court attorney presenting a case to a judge or, especially, a jury Lincoln was in his element, exploiting his formidable memory, his skill in questioning, and his stock of jokes and anecdotes. Writing in the 1870s, Isaac N. Arnold considered him the strongest jury lawyer Illinois had known, able to "compel a witness to tell the truth when he meant to lie." Lincoln, he said, "could make a jury laugh, and, generally, weep, at his pleasure." Swift to judge character, he "understood, almost intuitively, the jury, witnesses, parties, and judges, and how best to . . . influence them." His clarity in presenting even the most complex case, and his manifest honesty with the evidence, gave him a great advantage. So, too, did his "wit and humor, and inexhaustible stores of anecdote, always to the point," which "added immensely to his power as a jury-advocate."[55]

To Lincoln's use of humor in the courtroom must be added his entertaining conversation in the hotels and other meeting places in the county seats of the Eighth Circuit, where lawyers, jurors, witnesses, and suitors mingled with "singular comradeship." During periods of leisure the attorneys and residents would gather to swap stories; their evenings became "a contest of wits."[56] Lincoln's reputation as a teller of funny tales was second to none. Usher Linder, a fellow lawyer, recalled that wherever Lincoln went on the circuit "he brought sunshine. All men hailed him as an addition to their circle. He was genial; he was humorous." Another declared, "He brought light with him."[57] In an era when juries were not sequestered and jurymen mixed socially with lawyers, a genial attorney could gain advantage. Lincoln's capacity to entertain outside the courtroom gave him additional power within it.

In the political sphere, however, to which Lincoln returned with renewed energy in 1854, he would observe a much clearer line of separation between hilarity in private settings and earnestness in public. Stephen A. Douglas's Kansas-Nebraska Act of that year changed the complexion of national politics, by allowing slaveholders to carry their human chattels into western territories previously barred to slavery. For the next six years Lincoln set his political course by a compass fixed firmly on the true north of the Declaration of Independence and his conviction that the nation's founders had intended slavery gradually to die out, not spread. In this context, which included a revived political appetite for national office, Lincoln turned to public speaking as his chief weapon. The rhetorical strategy that he adopted marked a discernible break from what had gone before. The settlement of Kansas; the snare of Douglas's "popular sovereignty" doctrine; the grip of southern slaveholding interests on presidents Franklin Pierce and James Buchanan; the proslavery *Dred Scott* ruling of the U.S. Supreme Court: collectively these represented for Lincoln the most profound ethical challenge to his reading of the republic's purposes as set out in 1776 and 1787. A challenge so fundamental required oratory to match.

In consequence, Lincoln focused above all on presenting his case with an earnest mien that his audiences found striking. His aim was above all to convince, not to amuse, as he believed—from experience—"that it was doubtful whether turning the laugh on anybody really gained any votes."[58] From the eloquence of his defining Peoria speech of 1854, through his campaign speeches for the new Republican Party in 1856 and the rhetorical intensity of the joint debates with Douglas in 1858, to the triumph of his Cooper Union address in 1860, Lincoln's essential ethical-republican argument remained unchanged and his focus on it undeviating, even as the immediate political landscape shifted in the light of events. On a buggy ride to Greenville, in September 1858, Joseph Gillespie asked his friend why he was not using any anecdotes—a proven and potent weapon— against Douglas. Lincoln replied that "the occasion was too grave & serious . . . that in the discussion of great questions nothing . . . [extraneous] should be lugged in as a make weight."[59] Gillespie's question echoed the criticisms that Lincoln's various advisors—Joseph Medill, Owen Lovejoy, Norman B. Judd, Elihu B. Washburne, and Charles H. Ray—had made about the joint debate at Ottawa the previous month. They complained that their candidate "had been entirely too serious on that occasion"; he should "redeem himself by amusing the audience, after the fashion of the then celebrated Tom Corwin of Ohio." Lincoln would have none of it: "The issue was too serious to admit of jesting," he declared. (Corwin confirmed this hard lesson: "One of the most dangerous things to a public man," he warned, "is to become known as a jester."[60])

What puzzled his friends was the stark contrast between this unwonted public seriousness and the private levity that entertained them on their journeys between speaking appointments. Lincoln's tight rationing of funny stories would certainly have surprised Douglas and his supporters, who believed that his "droll ways and dry jokes" helped make him "the best stump speaker in the West."[61] The change was quite a disappointment for some. At Council Bluffs, Iowa, in

1859, fifteen-year-old Edward F. Test noted how the crowd had felt let down when Lincoln took his turn after a speaker who "understood the nature of 'the boys' and in his inimitable way told them a number of funny stories." Lincoln was too serious and argumentative for their taste. "Whether or not the fodder was placed too high for 'the boys' to get it, they said they liked the [other] speech the best."[62] Likewise, at the Wisconsin Agricultural Fair, Lincoln's earnest discussion of the claims of free over slave labor sent many of his audience wandering off "to the cow pens and sideshows."[63]

Yet Lincoln by no means shunned all humor during his joint debates with Douglas. Generally avoiding frontal satirical assault and name-calling, he made his thrusts more indirectly, often through self-deprecation. He pointed to the sitting senator's panoply of power, which encouraged his supporters to see in his "round, jolly, fruitful face" the rewards of office ("postoffices, landoffices, marshalships, and cabinet appointments, chargeships and foreign missions") "bursting and sprouting out in wonderful exuberance." By contrast, he said to cheers and laughter, "nobody has ever expected me to be President. In my poor, lean, lank, face, nobody has ever seen that any cabbages were sprouting out."[64] Mostly his humor found expression in striking metaphors or turns of phrase, wry comments, and witty rebuttals of Douglas's bogus charges and logical absurdities. Together they created the expressions of hilarity that, as the stenographers' reports reveal, regularly punctuated his speeches, and which were enhanced by his skill in turning the laugh against hecklers in the audience: "I never saw a man who could handle a crowd like Lincoln," one observer remarked.[65] At the same time, Douglas's occasional loss of temper worked to throw Lincoln's geniality into even more obvious relief.

Lincoln's colorful way with words inserted a vein of humor into his earnestness. A key line of attack mocked the incompatibility of Douglas's "popular sovereignty" doctrine with the Supreme Court's *Dred Scott* ruling: how, he asked, could territories ban slavery if slave owners had the constitutional right to carry their property there? He teased Douglas for his claim that, without active local support, slave owners' interests would be thwarted. "Judge Douglas has sung paeans to his 'Popular Sovereignty' doctrine until his Supreme Court . . .

has *squatted* his Squatter Sovereignty out. [Uproarious laughter and applause.] . . . He has at last invented this sort of *do nothing Sovereignty*—[renewed laughter]—that the people may exclude slavery by a sort of 'Sovereignty' that is exercised by doing nothing at all. [Continued laughter.]" What in substance did this leave of popular sovereignty? "Has it not got down as thin as the homoeopathic soup that was made by boiling the shadow of a pigeon that had starved to death? [Roars of laughter and cheering.]" In fact, he continued, "there is not even that thin decoction of it left. . . . The Dred Scott decision covers the whole ground, and while it occupies it, there is no room even for the shadow of a starved pigeon to occupy the same ground. [Great cheering and laughter.]"[66]

Douglas's capacity to protect himself by muddying the issues, Lincoln declared, was an art in itself. But he was sure that people could "see plainly that Judge Douglas is playing cuttlefish, [Laughter] a small species of fish that has no mode of defending itself when pursued except by throwing out a black fluid, which makes the water so dark the enemy cannot see it and thus it escapes. [Roars of laughter.]"[67] Equally, Lincoln used wry, gentle humor in self-defense. When Douglas, in a brazen fiction, called him one of the hard liquor folk of New Salem, Lincoln gently rebuked him for his "little follies." The Judge, he said to laughter, was "wofully at fault about his early friend Lincoln being a 'grocery keeper.' I don't know as it would be a great sin, if I had been, but he is mistaken. Lincoln never kept a grocery anywhere in the world. [Laughter.] It is true that Lincoln did work the latter part of one winter in a small still house, up at the head of a hollow. [Roars of laughter.]"[68]

More challenging, of course, were Douglas's charges that Lincoln was in league with out-and-out abolitionists, aimed at full equality between the white and black races, and sought to array "all men North in one great hostile party against all men South."[69] Here, too, Lincoln leavened the essential seriousness of his replies with gentle mockery. At Ottawa, he recalled that Judge Douglas had the previous month complimented him as a "kind, amiable, and intelligent gentleman," before rebuking "this tendency of mine to set the States at war with one another, to make all the institutions uniform, and set the niggers and white people to marrying together. [Laughter.]" Lincoln wryly confessed his "weakness" in welcoming "these pleasant titles . . . from a great man. I was not very much accustomed to flattery, and it came the sweeter to me. I was rather like the Hoosier, with the gingerbread, when he said he reckoned he loved it better than any other man, and got less of it. [Roars of laughter.]" Turning to the substance of his speech at Springfield in June, when he had used the words of Jesus Christ that "a house divided against itself cannot stand," Lincoln asked, "Does the Judge say it *can* stand? [Laughter.] . . . If he does, then there is a question of veracity, not between him and me, but between the Judge and an authority of a somewhat higher character. [Laughter and applause.]"[70]

Positioning himself as a potential Republican nominee for the presidency, Lincoln carried this fundamental mood of seriousness, touched with humor, into his round of meetings during 1859 and 1860. He covertly satirized Douglas in what was ostensibly a nonpolitical address, his "Lecture on Discoveries and Inventions," by characterizing "Young America" (expansionist Democrats who shared the Little Giant's appetite for Cuba and other territory) in terms that made clear his particular target: "Some think him conceited, and arrogant; but has he not reason to entertain a rather extensive opinion of himself? . . . His horror is for all that is old, particularly 'Old Fogy'; and if there be any thing old which he can endure, it is only old whiskey and old tobacco."[71] On another occasion, in a speech in Cincinnati, he drew on his gift for mimicry and "pleasantly repeated a mannerism of his opponent,—'This is what Douglas calls his gur-reat perrinciple.'"[72]

The speech that most powerfully asserted Lincoln's claim to national leadership—at New York's Cooper Institute in February 1860—could not have contrasted more strongly with his rhetorical mode of the 1830s and 1840s. Those who had known Lincoln for years remarked on his strangely inhibited platform manner. Instead of speaking "in so familiar a way, walking up and down, swaying about, swinging his arms, bobbing forward, telling droll stories and laughing at them himself," he stood "stiff and straight, with his hands quiet, pronouncing sentence after sentence, in good telling english, with elaborate distinctness," seeking to impress the newspapermen present.[73] In fact, the substantive thrust of that speech differed little from what he been saying for several years; what had changed was the weight of evidence that he now produced—after weeks of research in the state library—to argue that the nation's Founders were committed to restricting slavery as a means of its eventual disappearance. An address so purposefully constructed did not lend itself to gratuitous levity.

From New York, Lincoln headed into New England, seeking fresh ways of repeating the same argument but remaining true to the spirit of earnest moral engagement. Firsthand accounts describe a speaker who resisted any "attempt to raise a laugh by stale jokes" or "to 'stir up the groundlings' by story telling." A reporter in New Hampshire was won over by his goodwill: "He indulges in no flowers of rhetoric . . . ; he is not a wit, a humorist, or a clown; yet, so great a vein of pleasantry and good nature pervades what he says, gliding over a deep current of practical argument, he keeps his hearers in a smiling mood with their mouths open ready to swallow all he says."[74] His striking appearance—"a sunken-cheeked rack of bones" dressed in a creased, ill-fitting suit—was of a piece with his western accent, high-pitched voice, grimaces, gawky gestures, and homely images.[75] Where they exist, the verbatim reports show that Lincoln's addresses were punctuated by applause much more often than laughter and that what commonly prompted the merriment was his wry mockery of the ethics that sustained slavery. In New Haven he made much of the theologian who misconstrued the scriptures when a guinea coin was placed over a key word. So with slavery: "Whether the owners of this species of property do really see it as it is, is not for me to say but if they do, they see it as it is through 2,000,000,000 of dollars, and that is a pretty thick coating. [Laughter.]" Then there was the issue of the inconsistency of northern Democrats who agreed that slavery was wrong but denounced all efforts to restrain it. "Why are you so careful, so tender of this one wrong and no other?" The laughter reached its climax as he noted, "there is no place where you will allow it to be even *called* wrong! We must not call it wrong in the Free States, because it is *not* there," or "in the Slave States because it *is* there," or "in politics because that is bringing morality into politics," or "in the pulpit because that is bringing politics into religion; . . . there is no single place, according to you, where this wrong thing can properly be called wrong."[76]

When, rarely, he told a funny story, it was to make a similarly serious point. At Hartford, Connecticut, he found a graphic example to show that northerners who declared slavery a wrong were neither making war on the South nor threatening the Union. He was, he said, "reminded . . . of the man who had a poor old lean, bony, spavined horse, with swelled legs. He was asked what he was going to do with such a miserable beast—the poor creature would die. 'Do?' said he. 'I'm going to fat him up; *don't you see that I have got him seal fat as high as the knees?*' (Roars of laughter.)" To further laughter and applause, Lincoln added, "Well, they've got the Union dissolved up to the ankle, but no farther!"[77] Albert Blair, a student who heard him speak in Exeter, New Hampshire, thought he "must have sounded very odd to the precise easterlings." Addressing the fracture within the Democratic Party between "the imperious legalism" of the southern slave owners and the doctrinal "equivocations" of Douglas, Lincoln said the proslavery leaders' relations with the Little Giant "reminded him of a story" of a western farmer who on a bitterly cold night decided to freeze to death a troublesome dog by shutting it out. Somehow the dog kept finding a way back indoors. In desperation the farmer stayed outside holding the dog himself, waiting for it to expire. "But the dog was the better stayer of the two, and the farmer concluded to adjourn the killing until a more favorable season." Blair conceded that Lincoln's "peculiarities did not detract from the general effect. Above the grotesque and the humorous a lofty feeling was dominant," shaped by "the clear, earnest call to reason in behalf of human rights."[78]

By the conventions of the day, Lincoln's nomination as the Republican candidate for president kept him mute throughout the election campaign. Victorious in November, he remained publicly silent until his somber farewell to the inhabitants of Springfield three months later. During this time, as the states of the lower South passed their secession ordinances, he spent most days holding court in the Illinois statehouse. At these "levees" he would admit up to twenty visitors at a time for good-humored conversation. Henry Villard, reporting for the *New York Herald*, noted the president drew on an apparently inexhaustible supply of anecdotes "to explain a meaning or enforce a point, the aptness of which was always perfect. Though not a "brilliant" talker, what he had to say was "pervaded by a humorousness, and, at times, a grotesque joviality, that will always please. I think it would be hard to find one who tells better jokes, enjoys them better and laughs oftener, than Abraham Lincoln."[79]

That was about to change.

Washington, D.C., 1861–65

At every stop on Lincoln's roundabout train journey to Washington in February 1861 huge numbers turned out to hear him speak. Unwilling to disappoint, but even more unwilling to risk an impromptu address that might inflame the political crisis, he tended—at those places where he had no prepared formal address—to remain silent or make only the briefest of remarks. His natural gift for humor served him well. To excuse his brevity, he often prompted laughter by saying, in one form or another, "If I should make a speech at every town, I would not get to Washington until some time after the inauguration." Frequently, too, for lightness of touch, he experimented with a formula that by the time he reached Little Falls, New York, he had polished to perfection: "I have no speech to make," he said. "I have come to see you and allow you to see me and in this so far [as] regards the Ladies, I have the best of the bargain on my side. I don't make that acknowledgement to the gentlemen, (Increased laughter) and now I . . . am ready to bid you farewell when the cars move on." On occasions, he told an anecdote about a slow but sure-footed horse whose owner was a candidate for a county office with a good chance of being nominated. On the day of the convention he saddled up early, "but in spite of whip and spur, his horse lagged on the road, biting at every bush, and when he arrived late in the evening, the convention was over and he was defeated." So, Lincoln said, if he stopped at every station to make a stump speech he would not arrive at Washington until the inauguration was over. Telling this tale at Thorntown, Indiana, he laughed when the train pulled out before he could complete it; he was all the more gratified to find that some of that audience had followed him to the next stop to hear how it ended.[80]

In this prologue to his inauguration, Lincoln could not know how dark the passage of his presidency would be. Throughout the emotional turbulence of the next four years, humor would remain an essential ingredient of his private life, and would often surface in his business as well as social meetings, but it barely showed in the president's public addresses. Just as during the 1850s he had made a conscious choice mostly to avoid personal ridicule and satire in public, so now he made a similarly determined decision: to be "mighty careful," when "talking to the country," to respect the gravity of what was at stake by avoiding humor and vulgar levity.[81] Even before his inauguration, observers noted, "Abe is becoming more grave. He don't construct as many jokes as he did."[82] His first crucial speeches—his inaugural address and message to Congress in special session—were marked by an earnest appeal to patriotism and a sober explanation of why rebellion had to be put down; only some quaint expressions and an occasional touch of irony hinted at the author's underlying sense of humor.

When serenading supporters and musicians arrived at the Executive Mansion to celebrate a wartime success, Noah Brooks expressed surprise at the president's use of a prepared text instead of delivering a few impromptu words. Lincoln explained his caution: in some earlier offhand remarks he had "used the phrase, as applied to the rebels, 'turned tail and ran.' Some very nice Boston folks, I am grieved to hear, were very much outraged by that phrase, which they thought improper." At Gettysburg in November 1863, on the eve of his address at the new federal cemetery, he reluctantly emerged from his private quarters to tell a gathering of residents, "I appear before you, fellow-citizens, merely to thank you for this compliment. . . . I have no speech to make. In my position it is somewhat important that I should not say any foolish things." When a voice interjected, "If you can help it," Lincoln retorted, "It very often happens that the only way to help it is to say nothing at all."[83]

In the company of friends, colleagues, and visitors Lincoln regularly continued to take conversational refuge in anecdotes and jokes:

the habit was too ingrained and instinctive to change. But as president he was unable to enjoy with his cabinet the collegial merriment he had known as a circuit lawyer in Illinois—try though he did, to the uncomprehending irritation of Edwin M. Stanton, Salmon P. Chase, and others. The experience of war took its toll, and even when telling his stories the underlying strain was obvious. Sometimes he was so worn down that, Mary Lincoln recalled, "he spoke crabbedly to men—[Harshly so]."[84] Through overwork and nervous exhaustion, one of his secretaries confirmed, "his temper suffered," resulting in "a petulance entirely foreign to his natural disposition."[85] By the third year of the conflict visitors to the White House thought that the fatigued Lincoln resembled "a New York omnibus beast at night who had been driven all day" and that his eyes had "lost their humorous expression."[86] His friend Noah Brooks was struck by his physical change under the burden of office: "the hearty, blithesome, genial, and wiry Lincoln of earlier days" gave way to a "stooping figure [with] dull eyes, care-worn face, and languid frame. The old, clear laugh never came back."[87]

Even so, Lincoln's underlying good nature continued to impress those who met him. Unsurprisingly, his mood began to lift following the Union victories in the late summer of 1864. Receiving news of Philip Sheridan's successes in the Shenandoah Valley—a further boost to the earlier happy tidings from Atlanta and Mobile Bay—Lincoln leapt into an infectious round of jokes and anecdotes.[88] Reelection in November and the death rattle of the Confederacy further enhanced his high spirits. Following Lee's surrender at Appomattox, which heralded the swift mopping up of rebel forces still in the field, Lincoln rediscovered the unforced levity he had once known. On the carriage ride that he took with his wife on the last afternoon of his life, she told him she had never seen him "so supremely happy as on this occasion." "And well I may feel so, Mary," he replied, "for I consider this day the war has come to a close. We must both be more cheerful in the future; between the war and the loss of our darling Willie, we have been very miserable."[89] The treasury secretary Hugh McCulloch recalled that just hours before his death, he "never saw Mr. Lincoln so cheerful and happy. . . . The burden which . . . he had borne with heroic fortitude, had been lifted. . . . The weary look which his face had so long worn, and which could be observed by those who knew him well, even when he was telling humorous stories, had disappeared. It was bright and cheerful."[90]

Lincoln's untimely death would deprive the country of wise leadership during the process of national reunion and reconstruction. In a less profound but still regretted deprivation, the people lost a fertile and abundant fount of jocular stories. Still, he left a legacy that comprised, alongside a record of historic political achievement, a remarkable treasury of levity. His catholic sense of humor found expression in various species of amusement that invite examination in their own right.

SOURCES, SPECIES, SUBJECTS

L incoln possessed an apparently inexhaustible mental archive of jokes, comic stories, and wit. In part, he stocked it from his own reading and personal experiences, but at least as often he captured the best of the humorous anecdotes that he heard from others. Henry Villard found the stories Lincoln told "so real that it was hard to determine whether he repeated what he had heard from others, or had invented himself." Lincoln, however, claimed to have invented little or no comic material of his own, telling Chauncey M. Depew, "I have originated but two stories in my life, but I tell tolerably well other people's." In the same vein he explained to Noah Brooks, "I do generally remember a good story when I hear it, but I never invent anything original; I am only a retail dealer."[1] Where, then, does the credit for Lincoln's material lie?

Sources

Lincoln grew up in a semifrontier, rural society where storytelling was a part of everyday conversation. As a boy, Lincoln admired his Uncle Mordecai, an able raconteur, but within the family there was no more accomplished storyteller than his father. Thomas Lincoln was "very fond of a Joke or story & of telling them," according to Augustus H. Chapman, who had married into the family. Dennis F. Hanks, Lincoln's cousin, likewise testified that this was "one trait that Abraham inherited" from his father, who, he said, "could beat his son telling a story—cracking a joke."[2] Surviving examples of Thomas's humor are sparse, but he is reputed to have told his second wife, when she asked him if he liked her or his first wife the better, "Oh now Sarah, that reminds me of old John Hardin down in Kentucky who had a fine looking pair of horses, and a neighbor coming in one day and looking at them said, 'John, which horse do you like best?' John replied, 'I can't tell, one of them kicks and the other bites and I don't know which is wust.'"[3]

Lincoln's appetite for humor shaped his choice of company. His friends and acquaintances—on the land, in politics, in the court-room—served as an audience for his storytelling and as suppliers of comic material that he could customize for his own use. In New Salem, he found a congenial source in Bowling Green; in the Illinois legislature he discovered in an associate, John S. Hacker of Union County, an unequaled fount of funny stories.[4] Riding the judicial circuit for many years and stopping at country taverns, he would sit up all night with "lawyers, jurymen, witnesses and clients" listen-ing to "their life adventures."[5] As president-elect and then in the White House, he enjoyed the convivial and amusing companionship of Ward Hill Lamon. He relished even more the company of John Milton Hay, his young personal secretary; as the historian Michael Burlingame has noted, "Hay's humor, intelligence, love of word play, fondness for literature, and devotion to his boss made him a source of comfort to the beleaguered president in the loneliness of the White House."[6] Shaking the hands of visitors at a White House reception, Lincoln held up the line for a whispered conversation, to discuss not a great secret of state, as the company supposed, but the details of "a first-class anecdote." Occasional official visitors, too, supplied Lincoln's bank of material. Hearing an unfamiliar anecdote from a western senator, the president took down the details and filed them away in his desk.[7]

Lincoln regularly replenished his reservoir of material from his reading. In his earlier years he relished the humor in the poetry of Byron and, above all, Robert Burns, whose poems "Tam O'Shanter," "Holy Willie's Prayer," "Epistle to a Young Friend," and "The Cot-ter's Saturday Night" he committed to memory.[8] Aesop's fables, when embellished and adapted, served as pertinent commentaries on people and events (the fable of the disarmed lion and the wood-cutter's daughter gave particular edge to his critique of those ready to surrender to the extreme demands of secessionists).[9] The wit and humor of his preferred newspaper, the *Louisville Journal*, gave him special pleasure. He drew joy from the witty English essayist the Reverend Sydney Smith. As Lincoln traveled the judicial circuit he carried with him Joseph Baldwin's satirical sketches of legal life in the southwestern frontier of the 1830s and 1840s: the vernacular humor of *Flush Times in Alabama and Mississippi*, with its diet of long-winded comic tales centered on larger-than-life characters, perfectly served his appetite for colorful narrative. (Well thumbed in his copy was the preposterous earthquake story told by the unscrupulous, red-faced trial lawyer, Cave Burton, whose regard for truth was "so great that he spent most of his conversation in embellishing it.") Another of Lincoln's boon companions was *Phoenixiana*, a book of Californian drollery, whimsy, and absurdity by "Squibob" (George Horatio Derby).[10]

During the war years Lincoln took particular delight in the comic and satirical writings of three young "literary comedians": Charles Farrar Browne, Robert Henry Newell, and especially David Ross Locke. Each was a gifted storyteller who mixed irreverence, absurdity, and degrees of satire. Browne and Locke took on the characters, respectively, of an itinerant showman (Artemus Ward) and an ignorant, proslavery preacher (Petroleum V. Nasby), both of whom spoke idiomatically, wrote phonetically, and provided Lincoln with a low-brow text that, as a gifted mimic, he could perform as well as read. Newell's "Orpheus C. Kerr" offered a more refined assault on a variety of recognizable American types, including—as his name indicated—the class of political office seekers that also formed a target for the ridicule of Browne and Locke.[11]

Other sources of Lincoln's stories included one, possibly two, eighteenth-century English joke books. Some consider that he had sight of *Quin's Jests* (London, 1766), since its salacious anecdotes and wordplay have a kinship with what we know he liked, but there is also reason for doubt, as it never appeared in an American edition.[12] There is no question, however, about Lincoln's attachment to the stories, quips, and puns in *Joe Miller's Jests* (London, 1739), a copy of which was found in his desk after his death.[13] Judge Samuel Treat concluded that Lincoln had learnt the "entire contents" of Miller, having heard him telling the stories around the circuit, "but very much embellished and changed."[14] While defending a client accused of assault and battery, Lincoln adapted one of Miller's stories to illustrate the legal plea of *son assault demesne* ("his own first assault"). The defendant, he told the jury, had been legitimately protecting himself against the plaintiff's abuse and violence. His likened his client to a man who, when walking along the highway with a pitchfork over his shoulder, was attacked by a savage dog that had emerged from a farmyard. To protect himself, he stuck the prongs of fork into the beast and killed him.

"What made you kill my dog?" said the farmer.

"What made him try to bite me?"

"But why didn't you go at him with the other end of your pitchfork?"

"Well why didn't he come at me with his other end?"

Holding an imaginary dog in his long arms, Lincoln whirled it about and pushed its back end toward the faces of the comprehending jurors.[15]

Lincoln adapted another story of English origin to illustrate why, in late 1861, he ignored the proclamation of the army commander of Ship Island, General John W. Phelps, calling on the loyal citizens of southern Louisiana to abolish slavery. The president regarded the proclamation as an exercise in gesture politics: it threatened no measures of enforcement. "I feel about that as . . . Jones did about his wife," he explained. One day a friend of the meek and henpecked husband saw him being driven out of the house by his termagant spouse. "Jones, I've always stood up for you," he said, "but I'm not going to do it any longer. Any man who will stand quietly and take a switching from his wife, deserves to be horsewhipped." Jones, however, simply winked and patted his friend on the back. "Now, *don't*," he replied. "Why, it didn't *hurt* me any, and you have no idea what a *power* of *good* it did Sarah Ann."[16] In the original story, the husband was a lusty man capable of great endurance, while his wife was frail and feeble; Lincoln's adaptation added further comedy.

The Bible and the works of Shakespeare, his two constant literary companions, served Lincoln better than any other traditional sources in providing witty analogy and pertinent commentary on events. He knew great swaths of these texts by heart and could draw on them at will. An Illinois Presbyterian minister, observing Lincoln at the center of a group of citizens, remarked as he passed by, "Where the great ones are there will the people be." Without a beat Lincoln replied, "Ho! *Parson* a little more Scriptural; 'Where the carcass is there will the eagles be gathered together.'"[17] When the president's radical opponents called a meeting in Cleveland in May 1864, a week before the regular Republican nominating convention, to run John C. Frémont as a stalking horse for Salmon P. Chase, the expected thousands did not materialize. Learning that only about four hundred had been present, the president opened the Bible at the First Book of Samuel, to read, "And every one that was in distress, and every one that was in debt, and every one that was discontented, gathered themselves unto him; and he became a captain over them: and there were with him about four hundred men."[18]

On another occasion, a caller found the president "limp and careworn" after a visit from three radical Republicans—Charles Sumner, Zach Chandler, and Ben Wade—who had unsparingly urged the case for an emancipation edict. Lincoln remembered a classroom test from his childhood. He and his schoolmates had to take it in turn to read aloud from a passage of the Bible. As they progressed through the Book of Daniel, one boy was faced by the verse "in which Nebuchadnezzar in his rage and fury commanded Shadrach, Meshach and Abednego to be brought to him." The "jaw-breaking names were too much for him," Lincoln recalled, and as a penalty he had to stand at the foot of the class. When it again came to his turn, he saw the verse: "Nebuchadnezzar spake . . . unto them. Is it not true, O, Shadrach, Meshach and Abednego . . . ?" At this, the boy "dropped the book, stamped his foot in rage, and exclaimed: 'Here are those same blanked fellows again, and I can't read 'em!'" Lincoln said he felt just like that boy: "Those same blanked fellows—Sumner,

Chandler and Wade—have been here again, trying to get me to issue a proclamation freeing all the slaves before I am ready to do it.
I can't read 'em."[19]

Lincoln also illuminated his prose with occasional Shakespearean
allusions—sometimes as dry wit, sometimes in broad jest. Speaking
self-mockingly of a photograph that perfectly captured his "stiff,
ungovernable hair . . . sticking every way," he reflected that the
camera had been merely "holding the mirror up to nature" (*Hamlet*
3.2.22), with the result that newsboys selling the pictures cried, "'Ere's
yer last picter of Old Abe. He'll look better when he gets his *hair*
combed!"[20] More earnestly, when Stephen Douglas defended the
Kansas-Nebraska Act as a means of saving the Union, Lincoln scoffed
that it had "no relish of salvation in it"—a damning allusion to the
Prince of Denmark's words as he wrestled over killing Claudius at
prayer: better to wait until his sinful stepfather was drunk, swearing,
fornicating "or about some act that has no relish of salvation in 't."
Lincoln warned James Buchanan, after the Pennsylvania Democrat's
election victory in 1856, that as president he was the cat's paw of his
party and would be cast aside, unfit for further use: just as the Fool
characterized King Lear when his daughters turned him out of doors,
"He's a shelled pea's cod." Using less subtle, more boisterous and
misogynous humor, Lincoln summoned up Shakespeare's Sir John
Falstaff—that "tun of man . . . that stuffed cloak-bag of guts, that
roasted Manningtree ox with the pudding in his belly"—to paint
a cruel (April Fool's Day) portrait of Mary Owens, once the object
of his courtship:

> although I had seen her before, she did not look as my im-
> magination had pictured her. I knew she was over-size, but she
> now appeared a fair match for Falstaff; . . . when I beheld her,
> I could not for my life avoid thinking of my mother; and this,
> not from withered features, for her skin was too full of fat, to
> permit its contracting in to wrinkles; but from her want of
> teeth, weather-beaten appearance in general, and from a kind
> of notion that ran in my head, that *nothing* could have com-
> menced at the size of infancy, and reached her present bulk

in less than thirtyfive or forty years; and, in short, I was not all pleased with her. But what could I do? I had told her sister that I would take her for better or for worse.[21]

There is an echo here, too, of the grotesquely fat kitchen maid that Dromio of Syracuse describes with relish in *The Comedy of Errors.*

Although Lincoln appears to have jotted down a few stories, there is no evidence that he kept an extensive paper file of his comic material. It would have been strange had he done so, for this was not his normal way of working. As Henry C. Whitney explained, referring to Lincoln's legal practice, "In his exterior affairs he had no method, system, or order. He had no library of any sort . . . He had no clerk, stenographer; no letter-copying book, no scrap or commonplace book, no diary, no *index rerum*, no cash or account book, no day-book, journal, or ledger." As president, "when he wanted to preserve an unofficial memorandum of any kind, he noted it on a card, and put it in a drawer or, mayhap, in his vest pocket." However, "in his mental processes and operations he had a most complete method, system, and order; while outside of his mind all was anarchy and confusion, inside was all symmetry and precision."[22]

This system of working depended, of course, on Lincoln's extraordinarily retentive memory (or, as an army sentinel observed, the president's "awful poor forgettery").[23] Noah Brooks reflected, "Probably many people who heard him . . . repeat long passages from stories, or comical articles, . . . wondered how he ever found time to commit such trifles to memory. The truth was that anything that he heard or read fastened itself into his mind, if it tickled his fancy." Brooks occasionally tested Lincoln's recall by holding in his hand a copy of what the president was quoting, "and the precision with which he delivered every word was marvelous."[24] Whitney explained Lincoln's means of recall. "He gleaned quite as much knowledge from observation and by experience as anyone, but the crude product was passed through and crystallized in the alembic of his own mind and genius before it was of any concrete use to him. . . . Every material object or moral entity conveyed to him an object-lesson."[25] Lincoln himself put it more simply. When a visitor expressed surprise that he should spend time committing comic writing to memory, he replied, "Oh, I don't. If I like a thing, it just sticks after one reading or hearing it."[26] Another colleague explained that Lincoln "could recall every incident of his life particularly if any thing amusing was connected with it."[27]

Species of Humor

What was it exactly that touched Lincoln's funny bone? There is no single answer, for his sense of humor was unusually capacious and catholic. He relished almost every form of the comic. At one end of the spectrum, he drew pleasure from tall tales, absurdity, and larger-than-life characters: as Richard J. Oglesby put it, he "Laughed heartily at an ass."[28] At the other, he secured a certain cerebral pleasure in the plasticity, ambiguity, and surprises of language. There is no simple taxonomy or classification of Lincoln's humor, but between these two poles of enjoyment he appreciated a variety of other forms, and happily indulged in quick wit, irony, logical fallacy, satire, and—notoriously—dirty jokes and stories. Not least, like many successful and effective humorists, he knew how to win over an audience by laughing at himself.

Self-mockery

Lincoln, possessing a strong sense of self-worth, won praise for his ability to take a joke at his own expense, joining in the jollity "with the utmost innocence and good-nature."[29] He often elicited laughter through self-mocking stories and wit. Personal characteristics and habits that he might have turned to his credit—such as his abstinence from tobacco and alcohol—he chose to use against himself. He enjoyed telling the story of meeting a genial Kentuckian who had offered him a plug of tobacco, a cigar, and a glass of brandy. When Lincoln declined, saying he did not indulge, the gentleman remarked amiably, "I have gone through the world a great deal and have had much experience with men and women of all classes, and in all climes, and I have noticed one thing." What, Lincoln eagerly asked, might that be? That "those who have no vices," the Kentuckian replied, "have d——d few virtues."[30] Lincoln cherished the exchange and frequently repeated it.

Lincoln made much of his unprepossessing appearance. He told John Hay of a dream where he found himself with "a party of plain people" who commented on his looks. When one of them said, "He is a very common-looking man," he had replied, "The Lord prefers Common-looking people: that is the reason he makes so many of them." Hay noted that Lincoln thought this "rather a neat thing."[31] Conscious of his unusual physical proportions—his height and unusually long limbs—and aware that many considered him an ugly man, he faced that head on. Implicitly casting himself as the subject of the story, he related an encounter with a stranger in a railroad car, who said, "Excuse me, sir, but I have an article in my possession which belongs to you." Taking a jackknife from his pocket, the man explained, "This . . . was placed in my hands some years ago, with the injunction that I was to keep it until I found a man *uglier* than myself. . . . Allow me *now* to say, sir, that I think *you* are fairly entitled to the property."[32] On another occasion he reflected, "If I have one vice . . . it is not being able to say no! Thank God for not making me a woman, but if He had I suppose He would have made me just as ugly as He did, and no one would ever have tempted me."[33] He was similarly self-deprecatory when a photographer who was getting him to pose requested that he "just look natural," to which he retorted, "That is what I would like to avoid."[34] Lincoln's jesting gave rise to a yarn that when he was splitting rails while wearing only a shirt and breeches, he found himself looking down the gun barrel of a passerby who explained "he had promised to shoot the first man he met who was uglier than himself." Getting a good look at the man's face, Lincoln remarked, while baring his chest, "If I am uglier than you, then blaze away."[35]

He adopted this line of humor on the political platform. At a career-shaping convention of anti-Nebraska editors at Decatur in February 1856, Lincoln spoke at the evening banquet. He apologized for being "an interloper" at a meeting of editors, and encouraged them to think he was the subject of an incident involving a man with "features the ladies could not call handsome." While riding through the woods he met a lady on horseback. He waited for her to pass, but instead she stopped and scrutinized him carefully before saying,

"Well, for land sake, you are the homeliest man I ever saw."

"Yes, madam, . . . but I can't help it," he replied[.]

"No, I suppose not," said the lady; "but you might stay at home."

When the editors had stopped laughing Lincoln said he felt that "with propriety he might have stayed at home."[36] A weak echo of this approach featured several times in Lincoln's brief addresses en route to Washington in February 1861, when he used self-deprecation as a means of saying nothing of substance while simultaneously flattering his audience: "I may see you and . . . you may see me," and so, "I have the best of the bargain."[37]

Absurdity

Lincoln loved tall tales. According to Noah Brooks, he "thought that the chief characteristic of American humor was its grotesqueness and extravagance; and the story of . . . the soprano voice so high that it had to be climbed over by a ladder . . . made a permanent lodgment in his mind."[38] Russell Conwell wrote of being in Lincoln's company when a self-important man entered, whispered in the president's ear, and left. With a smile, Lincoln explained: "He tells me that twelve thousand of Lee's soldiers have been captured. . . . But that doesn't mean anything; he's the biggest liar in Washington. You can't believe a word he says. He reminds me of an old fisherman I used to know who got such a reputation for stretching the truth that he bought a pair of scales and insisted on weighing every fish in the presence of witnesses. One day a baby was born next door, and the doctor borrowed the fisherman's scales to weigh the baby. It weighed forty-seven pounds."[39]

Many of his tales were expressions of western ebullience.[40] There were men who fought themselves out of their own coats and into another; and the wife who urged on the fight between her husband and a bear—"Go it, husband! Go it bear!" In one of his earliest speeches for the Republicans in 1856, Lincoln told a tale of a young man from Tennessee. Riding on a country road, "mounted on a fine black racing horse," he was accompanied by a Yankee on "a rack-o'-bones of a horse, apparently hardly able to stand." The Yankee invited him to trade horses, claiming that his own was a highly valuable example of "the setter breed, which sets for big game as a dog sets for small game." Seeing a nearby deer, which the Tennessean had not yet noticed, the Yankee covertly used his heel to touch "his raw-bones on a tender spot," a signal for the horse to set on all fours. This, he explained, meant "there must be game nearby, for his horse never 'set' in that way except when on the scent." His companion, now seeing the deer, brought him down with his gun. So impressed by "the wonderful instinct of the horse," the Southerner at once swapped with the Yankee, "on even terms." Coming to a stream, the Yankee "crossed in good style." He looked back to see that the "setter horse" was largely submerged and its rider almost drowned. Eventually "reaching the bank and blowing water from his mouth," the Tennessean protested: "Here, you infernal Yankee! What kind of horse is this to drop on his knees in the middle of a stream?" "Hush! Hush!" replied the Yankee, "keep perfectly quiet. That's a setter horse; he sets for fish as well as for deer, and I tell you there's game there!"[41]

Several of Lincoln's extravagant frontier tales were adapted from well-thumbed jest books. *The Royal Court Jester* gave him the material for the story of Bill, a village drunkard, who got catastrophically intoxicated on a day of heavy rains, staggered down an alley, and fell asleep in a bed of mud. Waking at dusk, caked in dirt, he sought out the public pump to wash himself. On his way he encountered another drunk leaning over a horse post, which "Bill mistook for the pump and at once took hold of the arm of this man for the handle, the use of which set the occupant of the post to throwing up." Bill "put both hands under and gave himself a thorough washing," and made his way to the grocery. As he entered, one of his comrades, horrified by the sight, exclaimed, "Why, Bill what in the world is the matter?" "By God," he replied, "you ought to have seen me before I was washed."[42]

Learning in December 1864 that an army of John Bell Hood's forces "had been pretty effectually destroyed," Lincoln called to mind Bill Sykes's wolfish "yellar dorg" that preyed on his neighbors' food and animals. The usual attempts to shoot or poison the brute failed to dispatch him. In desperation, a man took a dried coon's bladder, filled it with gunpowder, and placed the bag in the scooped-out part of a cake of bread. When the dog appeared, he put a piece of tinder in the mouth of the bladder, set it alight, and closed up the cake with butter. The dog smelled the bread and swallowed it "at a single gulp." Soon there followed "a tremendous explosion, as if a torpedo had gone off under one of our gunboats. The head of the 'yaller dorg' rolled down the hill; the hind parts flew some distance, catching on a fence stake; the fore quarters fell on the porch; and intestines scattered around on the ground for a couple of rods." When a passing neighbor said, "Well, I guess you have got rid of that cussed dog at last," the perpetrator replied, "Yes, I reckon that *that* dog, *as a dog*, won't be of much account hereafter."[43]

Lincoln told a more cerebral but equally tall story of attending a meeting of the board of trustees of the Illinois Lunatic Asylum near Springfield. Aware that the building could be rather chilly, he put on his hat. As he made his way along, "a little lunatic darted out from a door" and exclaimed, "Sir, I am amazed that you should presume to wear your hat in the presence of Christopher Columbus!" "I beg your pardon, Mr. Columbus," Lincoln, replied, removing his hat and walking on. Later, after the meeting, and his hat again on his head, he once more met the little man, who said in severe reproach, "Sir, I am astounded that you should dare to wear your hat in the presence of General Washington!" "Pray excuse me, General," said Lincoln, obligingly taking off his hat, "but it seems to me that less than an hour ago you said you were Christopher Columbus." "Oh, yes that is quite correct; but that was by another mother!"[44]

Wordplay

There need be no surprise that Lincoln—celebrated for the craftsmanship, economy, energy, and idiomatic color of his prose—should have loved the humorous possibilities and curiosities of the English language. He enjoyed discovering particular usages and the meanings of words. He smiled at "the Dutchman's expression of 'somebody tying his dog loose.'"[45] When he found out the etymological root of "capricious" he remarked, "Now, that is very queer, and I shall never say capricious again without thinking of the skipping of a goat."[46]

On another occasion, a law clerk in the Bloomington courthouse, Luman Burr, saw Lincoln settling down to study the German language. Looking up, he said, "Here's a curious thing: the Germans have no word for thimble; they call it a finger hat (fingerhut). And they have no word for glove; they call it a hand shoe (handschuh)." There followed "one of Mr. Lincoln's inimitable laughs."[47]

Lincoln took delight in puns. He smilingly told the busy operators in the telegraph office that since it was a Fast Day, he was pleased to see them working so fast. He spoke of a son who, on being advised by his father to take a wife, responded, "Whose wife shall I take?" To Noah Brooks he remarked, "You have yet to be elected to the place I hold; but Noah's *reign* was before Abraham."[48] He memorized the phrase of the satirist Augustine Duganne: "Endymion Hurst, whose head, / Unlike his books, is red."[49] He once asked Judge John Dean Caton of the Illinois Supreme Court, "if it is true, as has been stated, that all three of you judges came from Oneida county, New York?" and, learning it was indeed so, prompted laughter with his reply: "I could never understand before why this was a One-i-dea court."[50] In court proceedings, Lincoln knew how to use a witty pun to advantage: an opposing lawyer who claimed that "he could bring a man to prove an alibi," heard Lincoln shooting back, "I have no doubt you can bring a man to prove a lie by."[51] More teasing was Lincoln's response when, during a break in a trial, Hill Lamon ripped the seat of his pants and reappeared in the courthouse with the damage unrepaired. A fellow attorney jocularly called on his colleagues to pledge donations for a new pair, but when the subscription sheet reached Lincoln he simply wrote, "I can contribute nothing to the end in view."[52] Puns often elicit groans, and this may have been Lincoln's aim when he said to Seward as they passed a sign for "T. R. Strong" on a Washington street: "Ha! T. R. Strong, but coffee are stronger." He invited a similar reaction for suggesting that because the laughing water in Minnesota was called Minnehaha, the Nebraska river "Weeping Water" should be named "Minneboohoo."[53]

In the same vein, Lincoln enjoyed playing with transpositions and what would later be known as spoonerisms. To a young man who asked about his family's historic roots, Lincoln replied, "I believe the first of our ancestors we know anything about was Samuel Lincoln, who came from Norwich, England, in 1638, and settled in a small Massachusetts place called Hingham or it might have been Hanghim."[54] Lincoln found pleasure in this passage, which he gave to a bailiff of a Springfield court:

> He said he was riding *bass-ackwards* on a *jass-ack*, through a *patton-cotch*, on a pair of *baddle-sags*, stuffed full of *binger-gred*, when the animal *steered* at a *scump*, and the *lirrup-steather* broke, and throwed him in the *forner* of the *kence* and broke his *pishing-fole*. He said he would not have minded it much, but he fell right in a great *tow-curd*; in fact, he said it give him a right smart *sick* of *fitness*—he had the *molera-corbus* pretty bad. He said, about *bray dake* he come to himself, ran home, seized up a *stick* of *wood* and split the *axe* to make a light, rushed into the house, and found the *door* sick abed, and his *wife* standing open. But thank goodness she is getting right *hat* and *farty* again.[55]

The passage is in Lincoln's hand, but it is not certain he composed it; at the very least, he enjoyed it enough to transcribe it.

When making his "rabbit tracks"—as Lincoln once described his compositions—he took pleasure in coining new words and using fresh terms to ensure crystal clarity.[56] A colleague noted how he described meddlesome people as "interruptious" and susceptibility to being duped as "du-pen'-ance"; he said of a man "who had been overtaken by a just retribution . . . that 'he had got his come-up-ence.'"[57] These terms were not all Lincoln's inventions: "come-up-ence" was first used in American legal circles in the late 1850s, and is unlikely to have been his coining. But, as William Bender Williams, the young manager of the Military Telegraph office in the War Department, noted, Lincoln had a particular appetite for colorful words, such as "skeered," "hunkered" and "by jinks." One afternoon the president hurried into the office with Seward: "dropping into the chair with shortened breath, he exclaimed, 'By jinks, we are here at last.'" Seward reprimanded him: "Mr. President you are swearing before these young men." Lincoln, "with a twinkle in his eye, apologized to us for swearing before us, saying 'by' is a swear word, for my good old mother taught me that anything which had a 'by' before it is swearing."[58]

Lincoln quite naturally took his relish for verbal playfulness into the political arena. Speaking in the House of Representatives in 1848, he ridiculed Lewis Cass's campaign biographers for puffing up their candidate's military prowess in 1812, and jestingly summarized Cass's role: "He *in*vaded Canada without resistance, and he *out*vaded it without pursuit."[59] During the 1858 debates Douglas argued that Lincoln's antislavery reading of the Declaration of Independence—to embrace both black and white races—was aimed at bringing about "perfect social and political equality with the negro." But this, Lincoln said to laughter, was "but a specious and fantastic arrangement of words, by which a man can prove a horse chestnut to be a chestnut horse."[60] He pointed out to Hannibal Hamlin, his running mate in 1860, one of the "strange coincidences" of their nomination: "the last syllable of my first name and the first syllable of my second name make Hamlin. So your name is inside of mine, and we should know each other."[61] In the short autobiographical sketch that he had written for Jesse Fell, to advance his prospects of that nomination, he ended, "If any personal description of me is thought desirable, it may be said, I am, in height, six feet, four inches, nearly; lean in flesh, weighing, on an average, one hundred and eighty pounds; dark complexion, with coarse black hair, and grey eyes—no other marks or brands recollected."[62] The final clause delivered a touch of dark dry humor: it was, as Walter B. Stevens noted, "the usual form in which legal notices of animals 'strayed or stolen' concluded in the northern states, while it was not infrequently employed in the South, especially Kentucky, for a notice of a 'runaway slave.'"[63]

Fallacious Logic

As a self-taught Euclidian logician, Lincoln took particular pleasure in the misapplication or subversion of logic. He relished the story of John Moore, an Illinois state treasurer, who was returning home one night inebriated "in a cart drawn by a fine pair of red steers." As they passed through a grove one of the cart's wheels struck a stump and "threw the pole out of the ring of the yoke." The freed steers ran away, leaving Moore sound asleep. "Early in the morning he roused himself, and looking over the side of the cart and around in the woods, he said: 'If my name is John Moore, I've lost a pair of steers. If my name ain't John Moore, I've found a cart'"[64]

Lincoln used a particular logical sleight of hand, long familiar to humorists, as a means of addressing the tariff question. He told of a fellow who had come into the grocery store in New Salem and asked for a few cents' worth of crackers. The clerk laid them out on the counter, but after just sitting for a while the fellow said, "I don't want these crackers, take them, and give me a glass of cider." So the clerk put the crackers away and gave him the cider, which he drank and headed for the door. "'Here, Bill,' called out the clerk, 'pay me for your cider.' 'Why,' said Bill, 'I gave you the crackers for it.' 'Well, then, pay me for the crackers.' 'But I hain't had any,' responded Bill. 'That's so,' said the clerk. 'Well, clear out! It seems to me that I've lost a [few cents] somehow, but I can't make it out exactly.'"[65]

Swapping tales with Major Thomas Eckert in the telegraph office, the president teasingly said that he only ever encountered the major when there was money to count. This comment prompted a seasoned story: the tale of a man in a buggy hurrying at night toward shelter to escape a downpour. As he passed a farmhouse, a man "apparently struggling with the effects of bad whisky, thrust his head out of the window and shouted loudly, 'Hullo! Hullo!'" The traveller stopped to ask what he wanted. "'Nothing of you,' was the reply. 'Well, what in the devil do you shout hullo for when people are passing!' angrily asked the traveller. 'Well, what in the devil are you passing for when people are shouting hullo!'"[66]

Lincoln knew how to use false syllogisms to humorous effect. Noah Brooks described an incident on a journey with the president to visit the First Corps of the Army of the Potomac. They rode in a jolting ambulance over a rough corduroy road. The driver, sitting well in front, "occasionally let fly a volley of suppressed oaths at his wild team of six mules. Finally Mr. Lincoln, leaning forward, touched the man on the shoulder and said, 'Excuse me, my friend, are you an Episcopalian?' The man, greatly startled, looked around and replied,

'No, Mr. President; I am a Methodist.' 'Well,' said Lincoln, 'I thought you must be an Episcopalian, because you swear just like Governor Seward, who is a church-warden.'"[67]

There was also fun to be had in the unexpected application of perfect logic. Lincoln was put in mind "of a party who, in speaking of a freak of nature, described it as a child who was black from the hips down, and, upon being asked the color from the hips up, replied *black*, as a matter of course."[68] In much the same vein was the story he told on returning to Springfield from the country. A fellow lawyer had complimented their landlord on the excellence of his beef. "I am surprised," he said, "that you have such good beef. You must have to kill a whole critter when you want any." "Yes," replied the landlord, "we never kill less than a whole critter."[69]

Wit

Sharp wit was not Lincoln's prevailing or most representative mode of humor: he is alleged to have said, "Wit laughs *at* everybody; humor laughs *with* everybody."[70] Yet Noah Brooks was far too sweeping in his verdict that Lincoln "was not witty, but brimful of humor." The truth was that Lincoln had a capacity for devastatingly quick wit and trenchant repartee. When it was observed that Attorney General Edward Bates had black hair but a white beard, Lincoln thought it "hardly could be otherwise": "he uses his jaws more than he does his brains."[71] To a dejected young counsel who told him that his case "had gone to hell," Lincoln replied, "Oh well, then you'll see it again."[72] After the diminutive Alexander H. Stephens removed layers of clothing on board the *River Queen*, the president remarked, "[T]hat is the largest shucking for so small a nubbin that ever I saw."[73] Gibson Harris recalled a group of loafers in the public square at Springfield "wrangling over the ideal length, in proportion to the body, for a man's leg." Seeing Lincoln approaching, they agreed to abide by his verdict. "'Abe,' called out one of them, 'how long ought a man's legs to be?' 'Well, gentlemen,' was the prompt reply, 'I don't pretend to know *exactly*, but it seems to me they should be long enough to reach from his body to the ground!'"[74]

These were gentle applications of Lincoln's wit, but he was not always so kindly. He characterized one of the Supreme Court justices as a "granny" who had lost his mental vigor, so that "if you pointed your finger and a darning-needle toward him at the same time, he could never determine which was the sharper." And of another judge, "famed for his close construction of the law," Lincoln said that "he would hang a man for blowing his nose in the street, but that he would quash the indictment if it failed to state which hand he blew it with."[75] Irritated by the length of a congressional report on a new gun, he complained, "I should want a new lease of life to read this through. . . . If I send a man to buy a horse for me, I expect to have him tell me his points, and not how many hairs he has on his tail."[76] And following the death of an Illinois politician of "overweening vanity" he remarked that had the deceased "known how big a funeral he would have had, he would have died years ago."[77]

Irony and Dry Wit

"Mr. Lincoln was quite humorous, although one could always detect a bit of irony in his humor," recalled Charles Adolphe Pineton, Marquis de Chambrun, who considered this quality to be of a piece with his poignant sadness.[78] Lincoln enjoyed the dry, ironic, and oblique wit that he heard from others, including the farmer who protested, "I ain't greedy 'bout land, I only just wants what jines mine."[79] He was a master of this form. Returning home after some absence and seeing the additional story built on his home while he was away, he asked a neighbor, "Good evening, sir. Can you—er—tell me—aw—if the widow Lincoln lives anywhere around in these parts?"[80] During a discussion of religious sectarianism, it was noted, the president "looked very grave, and made no observation until the others had finished what they had to say. Then, with a twinkle of the eye, he remarked that he preferred the Episcopalians to every other sect, because they are equally indifferent to a man's religion and his politics.'[81] Lincoln also used dry wit to deflate arrogance. To a young German nobleman who, desiring a military appointment, made much of his distinguished lineage, the president said, "'Well, that need not trouble you. That will not be in your way, if you behave yourself as a soldier.'" More gentle was a formula he used more than once when acceding to a request for a job: "The lady—bearer of this—says she has two sons who want to work. Set them at it, if possible. Wanting to work is so rare a merit, that it should be encouraged."[82]

Some of the most commonly cited of Lincoln's ripostes deployed dry wit of this sort. Judge Joseph G. Baldwin of California sought a pass to visit his Unionist brother in Virginia but met only refusals from Henry Halleck and the secretary of war. Securing an interview with the president, he pressed his case again, only for a smiling Lincoln to say, "I can do nothing, for you must know *that I have very little influence with this Administration*."[83] When a Kentucky state senator complained of Union military activity in Cairo, Illinois, Lincoln's secretary assured him that the president "would never have ordered the movement of troops complained of had he known that Cairo was in your senatorial district."[84] More celebrated still is a remark that Lincoln apparently made more than once in response to complaints of Ulysses S. Grant's heavy drinking. Congressman Henry T. Blow of Missouri visited Lincoln after the battle of Shiloh, to note that some were calling for the general to be replaced, fearing that he drank too much for high command. The president (adapting one of Joe Miller's gems) "asked with apparent seriousness" what brand of whiskey Grant drank "that he might send some to the other generals."[85]

Coarse and Indecent Jokes

Charged by his friend Charles G. Halpine ("Miles O'Reilly") to capture some new stories from Lincoln's lips, John Hay reported that he had been "skulking in the shadow of the Tycoon, setting all sorts of dextrous traps for a joke, telling good stories myself to draw him out." But, he lamented, "not a joke has flashed from the Tycoonial thunder-cloud. He is as dumb as an oyster. Once or twice a gleam of hope has lit up my soul as he would begin 'That puts me in mind of Tom Skeeters out in Bourbon county' but the story of Skeeters would come out unfit for family reading."[86]

Many—perhaps most—of the stories that Lincoln told were, as acquaintances politely put it, "not very washed" and "would not do exactly for the drawing room."[87] The vulgar, the earthy, and the off-color: these were a mainstay of his humor, remarked on by family, friends, and colleagues. An adolescent taste for smut during his early years in Indiana—encouraged by his cousin Dennis Hanks, to whom he sang "Little Smuty Songs"—remained a lifelong appetite.[88] J. Rowan Herndon alluded to "the vulger order" of the "Pranks he used to Play off when going to mill."[89] James Matheny thought "that Lincoln's mind ran to filthy stories—that a story had no fun in it unless it was dirty," and Henry Whitney agreed: "The great majority of Lincolns stories were very nasty indeed."[90] The pious Albert T. Bledsoe—later a Confederate clergyman—considered Lincoln "one of the most obscene men that ever lived," who "never enjoyed his jokes . . . with such a *gusto*, as when they were strongly seasoned with obscenity and filth."[91] William M. Cocke of Tennessee said whenever he "saw a knot of Congressmen together laughing I knew that they were surrounding Lincoln and listening to his filthy stories."[92] His tales were durable. Representative Moses Hampton of Pennsylvania, who served with Lincoln in the Thirtieth Congress, was struck by the story of "the old Virginian stropping his razor on a certain *member* of a young negro's body" and another about "the old womans *fish*" that "get[s] *larger*, the more it is handled."[93] Eleven years later, following Lincoln's presidential nomination, Hampton happily reported that he was "telling some of our friends about your '*Cocktail speech*' and sundry other anecdotes connected with your history in Congress."[94]

Aiming to sanitize Lincoln's reputation, several colleagues later emphasized that it was not the crudity that he loved so much as a story's pertinence and wit. Donn Piatt recalled some "very amusing stories, . . . no one of which will bear printing. They were coarse, and were saved from vulgarity only by being so strangely in point, and told not for the sake of telling, as if he enjoyed the stories themselves, but that they were . . . so quaintly illustrative."[95] Leonard Swett was certain that his friend's "love of the ludicrous . . . made him over-look everything else but the point of the joke sought after. . . . If it was outrageously low and dirty, he never seemed to see that part of it. . . . . It was the wit he was after—the pure jewel, and he would pick it up out of the mud, or dirt, just as readily as he would from a parlor table." Henry Dummer reflected that Lincoln told such stories only when they could deliver "a point with a sting to it."[96] Given the instrumentalist character of Lincoln's stories and jokes, these testimonies have the ring of truth. Lincoln's sense of humor was so well developed that mere indecency—earthiness without wit—held no charm for him. Herndon recalled "a person who so far mistook Mr. Lincoln once as to tell a coarse story without purpose. During its recital Mr. Lincoln's face worked impatiently. When the man had gone he said: 'I had nearly put that fellow out of the office. He disgusts me.'"[97]

It is impossible to establish the full range of Lincoln's indecent stories: concerned for his reputation, his friends were reluctant to record them. Lincoln himself saw the danger: when asked in 1859 "why do you not write out your stories & put them in a book," he "drew himself up—fixed his face, as if a thousand dead carcusses—and a million of privies were Shooting all their Stench into his nostrils, and Said 'Such a book would Stink like a thousand privies.'"[98] He was rarely tempted into public indelicacy. One example surfaced in his "Lecture on Discoveries and Inventions," where he described Adam's discovery of nudity and his invention of "the fig-leaf apron." This prompted a joking allusion to sexual union: "the very first invention was a joint operation, Eve having shared with Adam in the getting up of the apron. And, indeed, judging from the fact that sewing has come down to our times as 'woman's work' it is very probable she took the leading part; he, perhaps, doing no more than to stand by and thread the needle. That proceeding may be reckoned as the mother of all 'Sewing societies.'"[99]

Lincoln's "immodest" stories were more offensive to Victorian sensibilities than to those of our own time. This difference is surely true of a tale he told John Palmer Usher. A collector of relics heard about an old lady with a dress she had worn during the Revolutionary War. He visited her and asked whether she would produce the dress to satisfy his love of aged things. She did so, and he enthusiastically held it up, saying, "'Were you the dress that this lady once young and blooming wore in the time of Washington? No doubt when she came home from the dressmaker she kissed you as I do now!" As he did so—heartily—the unimpressed owner remarked, "Stranger if you want to kiss something old you had better kiss my ass. It is sixteen years older than that dress.'"[100]

Earthier stories dwelt on the workings of the gut. Abner Ellis, Springfield postmaster and merchant, reported a tale he had heard Lincoln tell about Ethan Allen. The Revolutionary hero visited England shortly after American independence. His hosts made fun of him and his fellow countrymen, "and one day they got a picture of General Washington, and hung it up in the Back House whare Mr Allen Could see it." When they asked him if he had noticed the picture of "his friend" in the privy, "Mr Allen said no" but added "it was a very appropriate [place] for an Englishman to Keep it," for there "is Nothing that Will Make an Englishman Shit So quick as the Sight of Genl Washington."[101]

Herndon himself recorded how he often heard Lincoln describe a fine party where a "man of audacity—quick witted—self possessed & equal to all occasions" was asked to carve the meats. The other guests watched him whet his knife. As he set about his task, "he expended too much force & let a fart—a loud fart, so that all the people heard it distinctly." In the shocked silence, he kept his cool and "with a kind of sublime audacity, pulled off his coat, rolled up his sleeves—put his coat deliberately on a chair—spat on his hands—took his position at the head of the table—picked up the carving knife & whetted it again, never cracking a smile nor moving a muscle of his face." With the guests wondering how he would escape his predicament, "he squared himself and said loudly & distinctly—'Now by God I'll see if I can't cut up this turkey without farting.'" The whole company, men and women, "threw off all modesty," collapsed into universal laughter, and cheered him for his audacious victory. "I worshiped the fellow," Lincoln declared. "The nib of the thing," Herndon reflected, was not its vulgarity, but its celebration of "audacity, self-possession, quick wittedness, etc."[102]

Lincoln used innuendo to jest about anatomy and sexual relations. Persistently asked by the Washington socialite Kate Chase, who had seen him "standing next to a wall up in an alley," what he had been doing, "he caved in" and said, "well, to tell the truth, Miss Chase, I went up that alley to shake hands with a fellow I used to know who stood up for me at my wedding."[103] When Mary Lincoln, attired in an evening gown, had her carte de visite taken by Mathew

Brady in New York in February 1861, the studio made multiple copies, which were stamped on the back "entered by Act of Congress." She sent one to her husband, who opened the letter, considered the photograph and the inscription, and remarked, "That's a lie—she never was entered by 'Act of Congress.'"[104] Years earlier, in Indiana, Lincoln had written a witty piece of poetry about an episode concerning one Charles Harper who "was going to mill—had an Extremely long wheat bag on the horse." En route he encountered the miller's wife, "who said to Bro Harper—Bro H your bag is too long—No said Bro Harper—it is only too long in the summer." The vulgarity led to a church trial.[105]

Lincoln confounded a cattleman, who had declared that lawyers' questions didn't scare him and that there were none he wouldn't answer, by quietly inquiring, "How long is your pecker?"[106] Herndon vouched for a story that Lincoln told when president, involving a boy of twelve or fourteen and his doting mother. Getting sleepy one day, the boy crawled into bed, where the house's large she cat joined him. When some visitors called by, the mother—as was her wont—began "eulogizing her fine, pretty and moral boy and at last to clinch the argument and have the boy exhibit himself in proof," she cried out, "Tommy—come out here, the ladies and gentlemen wish to see you." He kept still, despite his mother's call. She repeated her demand, "in her surliest tone." Grunting and rolling over, her vexed son "said sharply—'Mother—damn it—let me alone till I f—k this damned old she cat and get her with kitten.'"[107]

Leonard Swett and David Davis were more familiar than most with Lincoln's bawdy humor. Swett recalled a hot day when he and Davis traveled with Lincoln in a horse and gig on a long trip. Lincoln drove, squeezed between them. On arrival, Lincoln threw out the reins and told the livery stable man, "Put up that horse and let me get out of here quick. I've been sitting between a shit and a sweat." Swett also told of how they had visited the president just before the Union Party's convention at Baltimore in 1864. Davis was rather uneasy about Lincoln's chances of renomination. As the president ushered them out, he said laughingly that "you could never tell who to trust" and told the story "about a man and a woman in the old days traveling up and down the country with a fiddle and a banjo making music for their living." The husband "was proud of his wife's virtue and was always saying that no man could get to her, and he would trust her with any man who wanted to try it on a bet." One day he made just such a wager with a stranger, "who took the wife into a room while the husband stood outside the door and played his fiddle." He played "for quite a while" and at length "sang a song to her asking how she was coming along." She answered:

> He's got me down, he's clasped me round the middle;
> Kiss my ass and go to hell; be off with your damned old fiddle.

The story, Swett said, made Davis "mad as a wet hen." He burst out: "Lincoln, if the country knew you were telling those stories, you could never be elected and you know it." But the president just laughed.[108]

Satire

Lincoln took great pleasure in satire. From an early age he enjoyed wielding a satirical pen and never lost his admiration for clever writing of this kind. Because he "repurposed" his nonpolitical jokes and stories for political ends, it has been argued that most if not all of his humor was by definition satirical.[109] That capacious reading of the word *satire*, however, necessarily flattens out the degrees of difference within the range of political (not to mention private) purposes for which he sought to provoke laughter. Rather, for the benefit of distinct differentiation, *satire* is used here to indicate the assault on hypocrisy, ethical inconsistency, and double-dealing in people's thought and practice.

An early example is Lincoln's youthful exposure of the hypocrisy involved in the sexual double standard. Alert to the blind eye turned by society on a man's, but not a woman's, violation of the marriage vow, he crafted rhymes that echoed the sentiments of a doggerel poem he might possibly have encountered in *Quin's Jests*. James Matheny recalled a stanza:

Whatever spiteful fools may say,
Each jealous ranting yelper,
No woman ever went astray
Without a man to help her.[110]

The younger Lincoln's satirical, even reckless, personal attacks noted in the previous chapter—the "Chronicles of Reuben," "Sampson's Ghost," and the "Rebecca" letter from "the Lost Townships"—by no means exhaust the record of his anonymous or pseudonymous lampoons. One of the more cunning and dishonest of these was his assault, as much scorching as humorous, on the famed Methodist preacher and Democrat Peter Cartwright. Over the signature of "Samuel Hill," Lincoln published a letter in the *Beardstown Chronicle* in November 1834 that cast the frontier evangelist as a hypocrite for seeking to repair the "moral desolation" of Illinois by filling its common schools with Methodist teachers while at the same time attacking northeastern preachers sent by national societies for the same purpose; equally shocking, Lincoln insisted, was that both Cartwright and the interlopers had used their priestly power to bleed their churches for personal gain. The flaying of Cartwright was an exercise in grim humor, shaped by not only the young author's distaste for the Methodist's religious enthusiasm but also his desire to restrain the Democrat's political influence.[111]

No figure was more often the target of Lincoln's satiric pen and voice than his great political rival Stephen A. Douglas. Writing pseudonymously as "A Conservative" in the *Sangamo Journal* during the election campaign of 1838, Lincoln labeled the Little Giant a "man of expedients" who—"flattered out of his senses" by being dubbed a "towering genius" of Napoleonic potential—had entered a corrupt bargain to win the Democratic Party's nomination for Congress. On the same day his article appeared, Lincoln delivered an address at the Springfield Lyceum, "The Perpetuation of Our Political Institutions." Reviewing the recent countrywide upsurge in mob violence, he pointed to one of the lessons of world history, that "men of ambition and talents" did not allow their "ruling passion" to be constrained by routine political arrangements. The examples of

Alexander, Caesar, and Napoleon delivered one conclusion: "Tower-ing genius disdains a beaten path." When Lincoln put the question "Is it unreasonable then to expect, that some man possessed of the loftiest genius, coupled with ambition sufficient to push it to its ut-most stretch, will at some time, spring up among us?" no reader of the *Sangamo Journal* could have doubted to whom Lincoln alluded: the "towering" Douglas—all five feet four inches of him. The conven-tions of the lyceum prohibited political partisanship, but Lincoln had cleverly circumvented them through indirect satire. Two decades later he would use this tactic again, with his critique of "Young America" in his "Lecture on Discoveries and Inventions."[112]

After Lincoln's ill-judged satirical assault on James Shields in 1842, he exercised much more control in deploying this form of humor. In private, among his lawyer friends, he would occasionally "impale an object disagreeable to him on a sarcastic lance," and he lost none of his appetite for reading the satirical masterpieces of others, includ-ing the opening soliloquy of Shakespeare's King Richard III ("an utterance of the most intense bitterness and satire," as he described it) or the "genius" of David Ross Locke's assault on Copperheadism through his grotesque creation Petroleum V. Nasby.[113] But the pre-vailing tone of the humor that passed Lincoln's lips lacked cruelty and malice, and his satirical thrusts were in the main restricted to carefully constructed passages within longer speeches, notably in his contests with Douglas during the 1850s. That Lincoln had not merely learnt the lesson of the Shields affair, but had turned it to his advantage, is suggested by the impression he made on a radical German American who first heard him speak during the joint de-bates of 1858. Even while "attacking his opponent with keen satire or invective, which, coming from any other speaker, would have sounded bitter and cruel," Carl Schurz reflected, "there was still a certain something in his utterance making his hearers feel that those thrusts came from a reluctant heart, and that he would much rather have treated his foe as a friend."[114]

Several of those sallies rebuked the Little Giant for appealing to the racial antipathies of white Illinoisans. Faced with the charge that his opposition to slavery meant he sought full equality between the races, Lincoln mocked Douglas's fallacious logic. At Charleston he declared, to cheers and laughter, "I do not understand that because I do not want a negro woman for a slave I must necessarily want her for a wife. . . . I will also add . . . that I have never had the least apprehension that I or my friends would marry negroes if there was no law to keep them from it."[115] There was also a satirical edge to his reflections on color in a speech at Springfield: "I do not understand the Declaration [of Independence] to mean that all men were created equal in all respects. They are not our equal in color; but I suppose that it does mean to declare that all men are equal in some respects; they are equal in their right to "life, liberty, and the pursuit of happiness."[116]

Subject Matter

Richly varied as were the particular settings and subject matter of Lincoln's tales, it should be no surprise that in the main he located them in the places he knew firsthand: the early settlements and aspirational communities of the western states. In the case of stories and jokes with a British origin, he commonly adapted them—with added local color—to the rural and small-town American West.

Anecdotes connected with farming, hunting, fishing, and the rural economy loomed large. They featured almost all classes of western folk. There was the plowing farmer who dodged the challenge of embedded tree stumps by steering round them, and the blacksmith who, failing to shape a piece of soft iron into any useful tool, plunged the residue of white hot metal into a tub of water, saying, "Well, if I can't make anything else of you, I will make a fizzle, anyhow."[117] Lincoln told of the grocer, popular for his sausages, whose neighbor took revenge after a violent quarrel by throwing "two enormous dead cats" onto the grocery counter and saying, "This makes seven today—I'll call round on Monday and get my money for them."[118] The cast of characters included the barber who sliced through his customer's cheek and cut off his own finger; the keeper of a hotel who, to maintain its record of clean health, put dying guests out in the street to perish; the boatman asked by a boy to stop his raft for a minute while he rescued his apple from the turbulent rapids; and the traveler in a thunderstorm praying for "a little more light and a little less noise!" The tales featured quack or "steam" doctors whose ignorance threatened rather than saved lives, and the student lawyer who used gibberish legalese in his courtroom request that his opponent be challenged "with a *capias*, or a *surre-butter*, or something."[119] Drunks and gamblers provided their own additional color to this lineup.

Lincoln populated his stories with a menagerie of wild and barnyard creatures: donkeys, cows, sheep, and dogs, as well as squirrels, opossums, turkeys, lizards, and scorpions. He described the pony whose preference for cottonwood over oats and hay led him to gnaw his way out of a stable. He mentioned chin flies that kept plow horses lively, rabbits that were mistaken for skunks, and bullfrogs that were "nothing but a noise." There was the bear that turned on his pursuers, the young raccoon that the tenderhearted boy wanted to spare, the mare alleged to have run five miles in four minutes, the sow that had more pigs than she had teats, and the fleas that scattered as they were shoveled. Lincoln, who once joked "that he was an expert at raising corn to fatten hogs, but, unfortunately for his creditors, they were his neighbor's hogs," told of swine that in the hard winter freeze would have to root for potatoes or die. He recounted the sharp lesson taught by the case of the animal in the henhouse, surrounded by dead chickens, that denied being a polecat but looked, acted and smelled like one.[120] Lincoln relished the tales of the crows so frightened by a scarecrow that they brought back the corn they had stolen two years earlier; and the chickens that got so used to being moved that whenever they saw the wagon being prepared "they laid themselves on their backs and crossed their legs, ready to be tied."[121]

During the war years Lincoln's exposure to military personnel and practice gave him rich material with which to complement these rustic yarns. He joked about the greater expense of replacing lost horses than brigadiers, and drily estimated the rebels' strength in the field at "twelve hundred thousand" given the Union generals' regular complaints of being vastly outnumbered in battle.[122] He recounted the unconventional means he had used as a captain during the Black Hawk War when, unable to recall the proper command, he had got his company through a narrow gateway by dismissing them and ordering them to fall in again on the other side.[123] He told the story of the cavalry officer who had such a painful boil on his backside that he had to dismount while on reconnaissance but, hearing the blood-curdling war cries of approaching Confederates, leapt swiftly into the saddle and galloped to safety—thus discovering "that there was no cure for boils so sure as fright from rebel yells" and that "secession had rendered to loyalty *one* valuable service at any rate."[124] He noted the black humor of the legless soldier whose religious hospital visitor had left him a tract on the sin of dancing.[125] Particularly memorable were Lincoln's delicate words to a young woman whose deep interest in a hospitalized soldier led her to press the question, "Where were you wounded?" The infantryman, who had been shot through the testicles, repeatedly deflected her inquiry with the answer "at Antietam." Asking the president to assist her, Lincoln talked privately with the soldier and then took the young woman's hands in his own, explaining, "My dear Girl, the ball that hit *him*, would have missed *you*."[126]

Several of Lincoln's tales fell into the category of the ethnic joke—ubiquitous then, as now. These jests were populated above all by stereotypes of Irish and black people. The perceived folly and flawed logic of the Irish immigrant featured prominently. Lincoln told the tale of the officials in an Irish town who resolved "first to build a new jail; second, to build it out of the old one; and third, to keep the prisoners in the old jail till the new one was built."[127] During the era of the Know-Nothing surge, Lincoln asked his Irish gardener, Patrick, why he was not born in the United States: "'Faith, Mr. Lincoln,' he replied, 'I wanted to be, but my mother wouldn't let me.'"[128] When Lincoln was presented with a gold-headed cane and asked how he would know who had given it, he was told that the names of the donors were engraved on it: "What a fool," he reflected. "I am like the Irishman that went to the Post Office and when the Post Master asked his name sayed 'faith, an't my name on the lether?'"[129]

The supposed fecklessness and malleable ethics of the Irish also served as a target. Lincoln frequently offered the example of the Irishman who had taken the temperance pledge and asked for a glass of soda water, at the same time saying that he would be glad if the bartender would add some spirits "all unbeknownst to him."[130] Pat, the newcomer to republican politics, was eager "to vote early and late and often" and, when asked whom he wanted to vote for, "scratched his head, then, with the readiness of his countrymen, he said, 'I am fornent the Government, anyhow. Tell me . . . which is the rebellion side, and I'll tell you how I want to vote. In Ould Ireland, I was always on the rebellion side, and, by Saint Patrick, I'll stick to that same in America.'"[131] Lincoln once excused his overdue arrival at court by likening himself to an Irish sailor who was caught at sea in a heavy storm and who prayed, "Oh, Lord, you know as well as meself that it's seldom I bodder ye, but if ye will only hear and save me this time, bedad it will be a long time before I bodder ye again."[132]

Lincoln's jokes about African Americans included allusions to sexual prowess (the Virginian "stropping his razor on a certain *member* of a young negro's body") and played on the perception of un-educated black people as ignorant and gullible. In a society where very few white people subscribed to the idea of racial equality, there was nothing unusual about Lincoln's enjoyment of humor based on racial stereotypes, an embedded feature of contemporary culture that was reflected in another of his loves, blackface minstrelsy. But this appetite did not exhaust—or indeed define—Lincoln's understand-ing of African American capability. Quite apart from the pleasure he got from the satirizing of whites' racial fears (considered in the next chapter), he dwelt much more on the unexpected wisdom of ill-educated black folk, and on their natural wit and enterprise, than he did on crude references to their reputation for sexual power. The black preacher, Josh, admonished Joe to consider the awful choice between the road to hell and the route to damnation: "Josh, take which road you please," said Joe, "I go troo de wood."[133] A lady who had lost her pet poodle was overjoyed by his return but horrified by his filthy condition, the result of "a negro down the street [having] him tied to the end of a pole, *swabbing* windows."[134] Lincoln told of the wisdom of a black cook who, having fled the fighting at Fort Donelson, was asked,

"Do you consider your life worth more than other peoples'?"
"Worth mo' to me, sah."
"Do you think your company would have missed you if you
had been killed?"
"Maybe not, sah. A dead white man ain' much to dese sojers,
let alone a dead nigger. But I'd 'a' missed myself, an' dat's de
point wif me."[135]

Lincoln also described encountering, outside the Springfield railroad
depot, "a little darkey boy" named Dick, who was making shapes
with his toe in a mud puddle and said he was drawing a church, with
steps, front door, pews, and pulpit. "Why," Lincoln asked, "don't you
make a "minister?" "Laws," replied the grinning Dick, "I hain't got
mud enough!"[136] A British visitor, Goldwin Smith, recorded similar
humor when he met the president in November 1864 and heard the
story of "the three pigeons." The tale centered on "a negro" who had
been "learning arithmetic." Asked by "another negro" how many
would remain "if he shot at three pigeons sitting on a fence and killed
one," the student mathematician replied, "Two." "No," laughed the
questioner, "the other two would fly away."[137]

* * *

A further set of stock characters took a leading role in Lincoln's
repertoire. No one in his inventory of stories was more conspicuous
than the western preacher, no community was better exploited for
humorous effect than the rustic congregations those ministers served,
no moral frailties were more replete with comic potential than those
under scrutiny in the country meetinghouse. Frontier religion as
entertainment served Lincoln the humorist well. Just as significant,
however, was the opportunity it provided for satirizing the most
deeply conservative mind-sets—political and theological—in the
Union. As the next chapter will explain, nothing gave Lincoln greater
pleasure than the fusion of these two elements—the comical and the
ideological—that he encountered in a barbed, hilarious satire that
consummately assaulted hypocrisy and ethical double standards.

A JUST LAUGHTER AND THE MORAL
SPRINGS OF LINCOLN'S HUMOR

In the catholicity of Lincoln's comic taste it is easy to lose sight of what was arguably his chief pleasure: humor that elicited not just laughter or mere merriment but also *righteous* mirth—a *just* laughter occasioned by comic writing that delivered a moral critique. The evidence for this proposition lies in his appetite for a model of humorous writing that, by his own account, gave him the greatest and most constant pleasure. This was the sharply satirical work of a gifted young newspaperman, David Ross Locke, the imaginative creator of a corrupt and bigoted Copperhead preacher, one Petroleum V. Nasby. Locke's use of the egregious Nasby to ridicule disloyal opponents of the Union administration prompted Lincoln's unrestrained delight. "For the genius to write these things I would gladly give up my office," he told the author. His appreciation of Nasby exposes what can fairly be described as the moral springs of his humor. An expression of his lifelong appetite for anecdotes that centered on the religion of plain folk, Lincoln's pleasure in Locke's creation exceeded all other, thanks to the satirist's razor-sharp ethical edge.

Lincoln and Rustic Religion

Lincoln's taste for stories about preachers and religious enthusiasts has to be seen in the context of their ubiquitous presence in the western settlements. They were, as previously noted, among the earliest targets of his boyhood humor. The extempore, often hellfire, sermons of lay and ordained preachers, most of whom lacked formal theological training, provided a feast of opportunities for a youngster with a gift for mimicry and an appetite for entertaining others by taking the speakers' efforts to ludicrous extremes. ("When I hear a man preach," he would later say, "I like to see him act as if he were fighting bees!"[1]) In this he may have been expressing nothing more than the mere irreverence of the child, but Lincoln would never be at ease with the emotional, conversion-seeking strain in the various Protestant traditions or with their interdenominational warfare and theological brawling. The deistic rationalism of his early manhood would eventually give way to his seeking to comprehend, as president, the mysterious workings of "my God," but he never became a member of a Christian church or acknowledged the divinity of Christ. This context of unorthodox personal faith helped frame Lincoln's jocularity at the expense of the western preachers of salvation, their sectarian warfare, and the physicality of their religion (one Methodist minister got wrought up to such a pitch of excitement, he jested, that it was necessary "to put bricks in his pockets to keep him down.")[2]

Lincoln commonly placed his tales in a rustic setting of a log meetinghouse, or an outdoor camp meeting. Herndon's cousin recounted a story Lincoln told of his Indiana days concerning an "old Babtist Preacher" who spoke in an infested meetinghouse "way off in the woods" and in use just once a month. Dressed in coarse linen pants and shirt, the preacher mounted the pulpit and announced his text: "I am the Christ whom I shall represent today." A little blue lizard having run up inside his "roomy pantaloons," the preacher tried to slap it away, but to no avail: "the little fellow kept on ascending higher and higher."

> Continuing the sermon, the preacher slyly loosened the central button . . . of his pantaloons and with a kick off came that easy-fitting garment. But meanwhile Mr. Lizard had passed the equatorial line of waist-band and was calmly exploring that part of the preacher's anatomy which lay underneath the back of his shirt. . . . The next movement on the preacher's part was for the collar button, and with one sweep of his arm off

came the tow linen shirt. The congregation sat for an instant as if dazed; at length one old lady in the rear of the room rose up and glancing at the excited object in the pulpit, shouted at the top of her voice: "If you represent Christ then I'm done with the Bible."[3]

The folk who filled the congregations in Lincoln's stories were cut from a similar rustic cloth. He described the arrival of a Bible-selling itinerant preacher at "a rough frontier cabin, with children running wild, and a hard-worked wife and mother, slatternly and unkempt, not overhappy perhaps, but with a woman's loyal instinct to make the best of things before a stranger." Her hospitable welcome froze under the preacher's intrusive questioning and she "finally answered rather sharply that of course she owned a Bible." When challenged to produce it, however, she could find nothing. Eventually one of the children unearthed "a few tattered leaves." In the face of the visitor's reproaches she protested that she "had no idea that they were so nearly out."[4] Lincoln also told of a meetinghouse in Sangamon County where, in the days before newspapers, storekeepers took the opportunity to advertise a new line of goods before the preacher arrived. Two rival gunpowder merchants made competing claims, the first describing the quality of a new brand of "sportin' powder": "The grains are so small you kin sca'cely see 'em with the naked eye, and polished up so fine you kin stand up and comb yer ha'r in front of one o' them grains jest like it was a lookin'-glass." His indignant rival jumped up and told the brethren not to believe a single word they had just heard. He had seen the powder for himself and pledged that "the grains is bigger than the lumps in a coal-pile; and any one of you, brethren, ef you was in your future state, could put a bar'l o' that powder on your shoulder and march squar' through the sulphurious flames surroundin' you without the least danger of an explosion.'"[5]

Lincoln's rustic preachers were often ignorant and feeble. One was "a little wizened-faced man" who struggled to be heard as the people struck their tents at an Ohio camp meeting. He climbed the log pulpit, "and clasping his small hands, and rolling his weak eyes upward, squealed out, 'Brethern *and* sistern!'" (Lincoln imitated the piping voice to perfection.) Getting their attention, he continued: "I rise to norate on toe you on the subject of the baptismal—yes, *the* baptismal! Ahem. There was Noah, he had three sons—ahem—nam*lie*, Shadadarack, Meshisck, and Bellteezer! They all went in *toe* the Dannel's den, *and* likewise with them *was* a lion! Ahem." Amidst the crowd's cruel laughter he repeated his words, but to no better effect. He closed abruptly: "Dear perishing friends, *ef* you will not hear on toe me on this great subjec, I will only say this, that Squire Nobbs has recently lost a little bay mare with a flaxy mane *and* tail amen!"[6]

The comic possibilities of religious revival meetings gave Lincoln further scope. Finding himself with the support of only one cabinet member during a critical phase of the *Trent* Affair—when Britain threatened war over the Union navy's seizure of Confederate envoys from a British ship—he recalled the drunk man who strayed into an Illinois church and fell asleep in the front pew. He slumbered on as the revivalist asked, "Who are on the Lord's side?" and the congregation responded by rising en masse. When the preacher then inquired, "Who are on the side of the Devil?" The sleeper stirred, but not fully grasping the inquiry, and seeing the minister on his feet, he stood up. "'I don't exactly understand the question,' he said, 'but I'll stand by you, parson, to the last. But it seems to me,' he added, 'that we're in a hopeless minority.'"[7] Lincoln happily seized the legion humorous opportunities offered by such exchanges between preacher and congregation. James Grant Wilson, a Union officer, recalled the president's story of a southern Illinois preacher who noted in his sermon that the Scriptures told of only one perfect man, Jesus Christ, having lived on earth, and that they offered no record of a perfect woman. This prompted the intervention of a forlorn voice at the back of the church: "I know a perfect woman, and I've heard of her about every day for the last six years." "Who was she?" the minister asked. "My husband's first wife," came the reply.[8]

Inevitably, cases of slack morals and breaches of church discipline were ripe for comic exploitation. An Ironside Baptist, Deacon Slinker, when investigated for drunkenness, claimed he had taken no more than one mouthful of whisky on the day of the alleged offence. His skeptical questioner asked how much one mouthful was. In Lincoln's version, he replied, "Well, bretherin' and sistern I had a curiosity to find that out myself, and so I measured it, and my mouth hilt just a pint!"[9] Few stories gave Lincoln greater pleasure in the telling than that of a family of Adventists, the followers of William Miller, who during 1843 and 1844 had encouraged his followers to get ready for the end of the world and be lifted up to heaven. With their five children, the husband and his redheaded wife prepared for their ascent by agreeing "to make a clean breast of it to each other." The man told his wife to observe her marriage vow of obedience and to "own up first." "Well, Dear," she said, "our little Sammy is not your child." "Well," he asked, "whose is he?" "Oh Dear," said she, "he is the one-eyed shoe maker's. He came to see me when you was away and in an evil hour I gave way." "Well," said the husband, "is the rest mine?" "No," said she, "they belong to the Neigbourhood." In that case, said he, "I am ready to leave; *Gabriel blow your horn.*"[10]

Lincoln had little time for the theological contention between the various Protestant denominations, not least over the operations of God's grace and the limits to Christ's atonement for sinners. Whether salvation was attainable by all was a question that divided Christians, as was the matter of the means by which people could be saved. The theological spectrum ranged broadly from the high Calvinistic doctrine of the predetermined salvation of an elect, on the one hand, to the Universalist creed that all would be saved because of God's unconditional love, on the other. It was in this context that Cornelius Cole, Republican congressman from California, enjoyed Lincoln's tale of his early days in Springfield when religious life centered on the churches of three nationally powerful denominations: Baptist, Methodist, and Presbyterian. When a clever young Universalist preacher appeared in the community with the aim of establishing a church of his own, the settled ministers agreed on a plan to "preach the intruder down." The Presbyterian went first into battle. He reminded his hearers "how happily they were getting along in Springfield, spiritually and otherwise. 'And now,' he said, 'there comes among us a stranger, to establish a church on the belief that all men are to be saved, but my brethren let us hope for better things.'"[11]

Through these stories Lincoln revealed more than a glimmer of cultural affection for the rustic religious world of the western settlements. In the main the tone is gently mocking, with no sharp satirical edge. In the hands of David Ross Locke, however, many of the elements of Lincoln's stories—ill-educated preachers, vocal congregations, creedal doggedness, slippery ethics, and hypocrisy—serve a scathing politicoreligious satire, *The Nasby Papers*. As editor of the Hancock County *Jeffersonian* in Findlay, Ohio, Locke fathered a grotesque: a proslavery Copperhead pastor whose illiterate columns first appeared in April 1862. Petroleum V. Nasby's middle initial stood for "Vesuvius," a signal for his readers to steady themselves for regular, caustic eruptions on the pressing issues of the day. Nasby was a selfish and conniving political office seeker: dissolute, whisky-drinking, red-nosed, greedy, loud, unprincipled, bigoted, hypocritical, dissembling, and sordid. The residents of Findlay, according to Locke's modern biographer, speculated on the inspiration for the villain. In the town's tavern a man once asked Locke, "Just what kind of a man is Nasby, really, as you write him?" The editor allegedly replied, "He's something like you—a sort of nickel-plated son of a bitch."[12] Nasby's villainy was impregnable. To understand why Lincoln found the satire so powerful and immensely satisfying calls for an examination of Locke's creation and the world the satirist aimed to expose.

The Copperheads' Moral Order

Locke's caustic satire delivered a devastating critique of the Peace Democrats' religion and the ethical perspectives it endorsed. Copperheads enjoyed some support within most denominational families. They included Irish and German Catholic voters, and in many parts of the lower North and the border area, antimission Baptists, old-school Presbyterians, and Disciples harbored significant pro-southern sentiment. Deep conservatism shaped their assault on what they saw as unscriptural Puritan meddling in the lives of others through campaigns for moral and social reform. They drew on a cluster of theological and moral arguments: the presumptuousness of human effort in the face of God's sovereignty and predetermined plan for the world; the primacy and privacy of personal devotion; the mistaking of political platforms for religious truth.

In particular, they defended slavery as a scriptural institution, legitimized by the practices of the Old Testament patriarchs and by the "curse of Ham" (Noah's curse on Ham's son Canaan to be "a servant of servants"). The account of the Egyptian slave girl, Hagar, who ran away after conceiving a child by Abraham but who returned at the command of an angel of the Lord, gave the defenders of the Fugitive Slave Law a handy text, as did Paul's instructing the run-away slave Onesimus to return to his master.[13] They deemed slavery consistent with natural justice; it was only its abuses that should exercise Christians. Copperhead religion consequently provided moral grounding for the deep racial antipathies of those white northerners who bewailed "a vulgar and brutal quarrel about negroes" and berated Lincoln for "striving to make the war a conflict between the white and black race. . . . How long will the caucasian man allow this blasphemy to go out to the nations that 'God and the negro are to save the Republic!'"[14]

Their moral anguish became all the more vocal as Union military campaigns evolved into a hard war against southern civilians and their property, and as black troops took their place in the Federal front line. Pious Democrats condemned the administration, and the pulpit that sustained it, for their bloodthirstiness: "Instead of feeding your people with 'the bread of life,' you feed them with blood and gunpowder."[15] Copperhead Christian pacifism was tactical and contingent, not fundamental, but it struck a chord with those troubled by the sanguinary language of their pious opponents.

A further religious indictment of the Union leadership was its assault on constitutional rights. Moral fury shaped the torrent of criticism that engulfed the administration for suspending habeas corpus, relying on military courts, and closing disloyal newspapers. Opponents charged Lincoln with a sacrilegious betrayal of America's God-given role as the repository of individual freedom, civil and spiritual. "Mobs, bastiles [sic], suspensions of the Courts, arbitrary arrests, destruction of democratic newspapers, and all the old fashioned machinery of despotism," one Copperhead declared, "have sufficiently attested that this is a war of Puritanism against the free institutions established by our Revolutionary fathers." Fusing fidelity to God and to the Constitution, these critics found their most celebrated Christian martyr in Congressman Clement Vallandigham, who, following his military arrest for disloyalty, was subsequently banished to the Confederacy.[16]

Lincoln himself took a prime place in the demonology of pious Democrats. His calling of days for fasting and thanksgiving made him an agent of "meddlesome, domineering and intolerant" Puritanism.[17] "[S]teeped in vulgarity and obscenity," he had spread a "foetid moral atmosphere" across the land and had "Sodomized the nation," tolerating the Federal armies' complicity in rape and racial mixing. His character spoke through his face—that "of a demon, cunning, obscene, treacherous, lying, and devilish." In the imaginative satire of Chauncey Burr, the editor of the *Old Guard*, Lincoln appeared as a satanic wizard, directing three devil-possessed Shakespearean witches: the secretaries of state, war, and the treasury—Seward, Stanton, and Chase.[18]

Locke's Nasby

David Ross Locke was one of those "meddlesome, domineering and intolerant" Puritans who so alarmed the Copperheads. Born in upstate New York in 1833, he moved to Ohio at the age of twenty. There he edited a succession of small-town papers, championing antislavery and the infant Republican Party. He bought the *Hancock Jeffersonian* of Findlay, Ohio, in 1861.

Locke's earliest Nasby letters establish his creation—an inhabitant of the fictional Ohio village crossroads Wingert's Corners—as the determined enemy of reform, abolition, and progressive causes. To escape the Union draft, he takes refuge in Canada. Returning home, he is seized and conscripted. He flees to the Confederacy and enlists in an infantry regiment, the Louisiana Pelicans. Disillusioned with the straitened conditions of Confederate service, he again returns home, is arrested for desertion, and imprisoned. Returning to Wingert's Corners on his release, Nasby organizes a Democratic church through whose pulpit for the rest of the war he preaches the antiblack, proslavery peace gospel of "St Valandygum."

Locke's biting satire was designed to arouse an indignant patriotism through pungent coarseness. One scholar has described Nasby's
papers as "the Civil War etched in sulphuric acid."[19] They won a huge
and devoted readership in Republican newspapers well beyond Ohio.
The *Philadelphia North American* believed that Nasby "puts both rebel
and copperhead arguments on the public green with a drapery so thin
that every deformity shows through."[20] Charles Sumner later deemed
the papers "[u]nquestionably . . . among the influences and agencies
by which disloyalty in all its forms was exposed, and public opinion
assured on the right. It is impossible to measure their value." More
pithily, the commissioner of internal revenue, George S. Boutwell,
deemed Union victory attributable to three forces: the Army, the
Navy, and the Nasby letters.[21]

What was it that readers so admired? In part, the letters fed an
appetite for rustic and burlesque comedy through a grotesque creation, more gargoyle than human being. But what gave Nasby the
edge over Artemus Ward, Orpheus C. Kerr, and others was Locke's
devastating satirical voice and uncompromising ethical critique. Like
all memorable satire, Nasby's letters stake out a conflict between two
worldviews, one explicit and ridiculed by the use of the *reductio ad
absurdum*, the other implicit. Nasby was the negative photographic
print which, when reversed, yielded the positive moral order. The
author's implicit voice was that of the New England Puritan moralist.
Locke was not deeply religious, but he deplored slavery and was as
close to a racial egalitarian as one could find among white Americans of his time. At the core of his astringent satire is a concern for
justice in the face of racial bigotry and a crusade against the version
of Christianity that sustained it.[22]

Nasby's genesis lay in the wartime circumstances facing Union
loyalists in the lower North and border: deep anxiety, split communities, and proximate violence. Years later Locke explained how the
strain of war compelled him to "write strong."

Imagine a town of 2000 inhabitants sending out a company of
100 of her bravest young men. . . . Imagine of that 100, 65 killed
in one afternoon. Imagine the black pall that spread over that

town as one by one, the telegraph ticked off the names of the dead. Imagine the streets filled with hair disheveled, shrieking mothers, wives, sisters and sweethearts. Imagine the marble-faced fathers and brothers, friends. . . . If you can imagine this, you can get an idea of what I saw in an Ohio town in '62. Write strong? We lived a year each day from '61 to '65.[23]

It was here—in this white-hot crucible of strife, anxiety, and mutual suspicion—that Nasby saw the light of day.

Locke's appalling creation generated its satirical power by means of the moral universe Nasby inhabited and the deformed piety with which he sanctified it. He was installed as the pastor of "a strikly Dimekratic Church" at Wingert's Corners in June 1862: the "Church uv St Valandygum," it would later reach its apotheosis as the "Church of the Noo Dispensashun." The antithesis of the self-improving New England Protestant, Nasby is fundamentally feckless and lazy (his church exercises require that "People assemble at the second tootin uv the horn"). Addicted to tobacco and whisky, he gives himself dispensation from the rules relating to fast days ("void in the case uv peepil over 35 and invalids, who may hev their sustainin flooids ez usual"). He labels his pastoral work the "apossel biznis" and plunders his congregation by coercion and outright cheating. Unembarrassed greed has him hankering after lucrative political jobs, above all the plum of a "post orifis."[24]

Locke uses his creation to rebuke the routine hypocrisy of Democrats who attacked the "political" preaching of Unionist clergy. Nasby the preacher sanctifies resistance to the arrest of southern sympathizers, to the draft, and to "Evrything the Administrashen hez dun, is doin, er may hereafter do." Adamant in his "unfaltrin trust in the rychusnis uv the Suthrin coz," he "viggerously" encourages the "mobbin uv Methodis, Presbyterin, Luthrin, Brethrin and uther hetrodox churchis."[25]

The motors that drive Nasby's religion and politics are proslavery fervor and racial animus ("a holesum prejoodis agin evrything black"). He begins his services with the reading of scriptural passages "provin that niggers is Skriptoorally slaves, and . . . the Fugitive Slave Law to be skriptooral." However, he adds, "The rest uv the Bible we consider figgerative, and pay no attenshun to, whatever." He exploits the fear of fugitive slaves' migration from the South and the threat to white labor. He cooks up preposterous numbers of black people settling in Ohio. Making hay with the internal contradictions in the Copperhead argument, Locke has Nasby address serving white soldiers on the danger of shiftless incomers who "hev seezed upon yure labor [while] you air taxt by a nigger-luvin Government to support them in idlenis." Nasby fulminates equally against miscegenation—the races' sexual mixing—and demands "the niggers be druv out": "A rowse to-wunst! Rally agin Conway! Rally agin Sweet! Rally agin Hegler! Rally agin Hegler's family! Rally agin the porter at the Reed House! Rally agin the cook at the Crook House! Rally agin the nigger wider in Vance's addition! Rally agin Missis Umstid! Rally agin Missis Umstid's childern by her first husband! Rally agin Missis Umstid's childern by her sekkund husband! Rally agin all the rest uv Missis Umstid's childern! Rally agin the nigger that kum yesterday! Rally agin the saddle-kulurd girl that yoost 2 be hear! Ameriky fer white men!"[26]

Locke, the racial egalitarian, uses Nasby's uninhibited and exuberant recourse to the word *nigger* to ridicule its ubiquity in Democrats' political rhetoric and highlight the Copperheads' obsession—near monomania—with race. Reflecting on how "Dimocrisy" could best keep the people "strung up the proper pitch," Nasby concludes, "Nigger is all the capital we hev left."[27] Locke, however, meant to shock as well as amuse. The northern social elite generally considered the word *nigger* a crude and derogatory term that degraded both user and subject.

Lincoln and Nasby

Nasby found no more avid reader than the president himself. Locke had first spoken with Lincoln "without reserve" in Quincy, Illinois, during the senatorial campaign of 1858; he would meet with him again the following year and twice during the war, in 1863 and 1864.[28] Lincoln prompted the first of those White House meetings by sending an invitation that amused Locke for its "reckless generosity, and the caution which followed close at its heels." "Why don't you come to Washington and see me?" the president had written. "Is there no place you want? Come on and I will give you any place that you ask for—*that you are capable of filling—and fit to fill.*" Locke went, though not to solicit a post. He found the president a regular reader of and "very much pleased" with the Nasby letters. If Locke's recollection is accurate, then Lincoln must have begun reading them in the newspaper press before some three dozen pieces appeared in pamphlet form in 1864. That collection, Locke recalled, the president kept "in a drawer in his table, and it was his wont to read them on all occasions to his visitors, no matter who they might be, or what their business was. He seriously offended many of the great men of the Republican Party in this way. Grave and reverend Senators who came charged to the brim with important business . . . took it ill that the President should postpone the consideration thereof while he read them a letter."[29]

Not only senators took offense. When the president read Nasby—"*con amore*"—to Edwin M. Stanton and Charles A. Dana as they waited for the October 1864 election returns at the telegraph office, the secretary of war grew increasingly impatient. With the arrival of the equally humorless Chase, Stanton pulled Dana into an adjoining room and exploded: "God damn it to hell. Was there ever such nonsense? Was there ever such an inability to appreciate what is going on in an awful crisis? Here is the fate of this whole republic at stake, and here is the man around whom it all centers, on whom it all depends, turning aside from this monumental issue to read the God damned trash of a silly mountebank!"[30] Dana himself recalled Stanton's indignation: "The idea that when the safety of the Republic was thus at issue . . . the leader . . . could turn aside to read such balderdash and to laugh at such frivolous jests, was to his mind something most repugnant and damnable."[31]

Locke was, in Charles Sumner's words, Lincoln's "favorite humorist," a verdict given substance during the senator's visit to the White House in March 1865. As the two men dealt with a matter of some seriousness (the judgment of a court-martial), Lincoln quoted Nasby from memory. Sensing Sumner was at a loss, he offered to "initiate" him and repeated the tribute he had previously delivered to Locke himself: "For the genius to write these things I would gladly give up my office."[32] Pulling out the pamphlet of Nasby letters from his desk, Sumner recalled, Lincoln "proceeded to read from it with infinite zest, while his melancholy features grew bright. It was a delight to see him surrender so completely to the fascination." Although there were some thirty people waiting in the antechamber, some of high political rank, Lincoln went on reading for twenty minutes or more, and would have gone on longer had not Sumner tactfully drawn this "lesson of the morning" to a close. The copy of *The Nasby Papers* from which the president recited with such appetite was in all likelihood the pamphlet later lodged in the Library of Congress—known to have been Lincoln's personal copy, whose candlelight singeing testifies to its being Lincoln's night-time companion and comforter. Nasby was so much a staple of his reading that Leonard Swett, his close friend, believed the president read him "as much as he did the Bible."[33]

What was it that Lincoln so admired in Locke's creation? He has left no explicit statement. But we may draw some inferences. As already noted, vulgar and enthusiastic preaching that appealed more to the heart than to the head had long prompted his laughter. Lincoln would certainly have delighted in Locke's echoes of the tub-thumping sermon built on a mercilessly repeated text. Nasby is the epitome of ignorance, drawing his verses from such concoctions as the books of "Joab" and "Abiram." He compliments his congregation for smiting an enrolling officer "hip and thigh, even ez Bohash smote Jaheel." He has the cadences of the practiced preacher, but instead of gravitas there is bathos. Urging his flock to copy the Israelites' blowing of rams' horns and flatten the walls of the "Abolishn Gerryko," he tells them, "Blow your horns, my brethren, for whoso bloweth not his own horn the same shall not be blown, but whoso bloweth his own horn the same shall be blown with a muchness."[34]

Some of the appeal of Locke's humor lies in his verbal inventiveness: his contrived misspellings, spoof dialect, wild grammar, misquotations, and a "shattered orthography" that presages today's text messaging.[35] This creativity certainly played to Lincoln's taste, noted earlier, for linguistic tricks, and just as parodies of scripture drew a chuckle so surely would Nasby's mangling of Shakespeare.

"Adoo, vane world, ado! I'll be a nunnery," he declares on learning of Vallandigham's banishment.

Then, too, there is absurdity of gothic proportions. When Nasby visited Camp Dennison to electioneer for Vallandigham, he "wuz pelted with offensiv eggs, and rotten cabbig, and decayed pertaters, in fact at wun time the air wuz so full uv eggs, that I might hev thot, hed I bin poetikle, that the blessid sun wuz a mammoth hen, badly diseazd, and a layin rotten eggs a milyun a minnit." Equally silly is Nasby's lengthy and self-contradictory catalog of "fizzekle" defects that must prevent his military service: he suffers from bald-headedness and dandruff, "kronic diarrear and kostivness." Absurdly implausible, too, is his listing of church members as they face the draft[36]:

Hole number uv male members	200
Over 45	50
Under 18	50
Badly rupcherd, and utherwise diseasd	92
Gone to Canady 2 visit their uncles	8

Nasby also provided a vehicle for simple jokes. Reflecting on the unbridgeable chasm between war and peace Democrats, Nasby is reminded of the "spritely boy" who put 200 eggs in a nest for a hen to sit on. "Sez his maternal mother, 'My son why puttist thou so many eggs under the hen. She cannot kiver em.' 'Certainly she canst not,' [replies the son] 'but thunder, I want to see her spread herself.' Jest so. . . . The outside egg in the Dimekratik nest is opposition to the war. Tother side uv the nest 200 eggs distant, is the support uv the war. To kiver em all requires great stretchin capacity."[37]

But what above all appealed to Lincoln, in Locke's judgment, was the savagery of the satire. Locke declared that Lincoln's satirical sense "was at times as blunt as a meat-ax, and at others as keen as a razor," and he located its inspiration (and its most "terrible" expression) in Lincoln's hatred of "horrible injustice. . . . Weakness he was never ferocious with, but intentional wickedness he never spared." In identifying Lincoln's appreciation of the Nasby papers in their assault on injustice, Locke recognized a close kinship with his own values and political impulses. If, as Russell Conwell would recall, Lincoln told him that "the devil cannot bear a good joke," then satire was a weapon whose power increased in proportion to the depth of the wrong it addressed.[38]

From his campaigning experience, especially in lower Illinois, Lincoln knew well enough the rural Copperhead Democrat type whose commitment to continued African American enslavement challenged his profound sense of justice. If there is one mantra that consistently stands out among the recollections of Lincoln's friends and closest acquaintances, it is of his being guided by the pole star of justice. This was no posthumous discovery shaped by hero worship or sentimentalism. Herndon told Henry Wilson in 1860 that Lincoln "loves all mankind—hates Slavery—every form of Despotism. Put these together—Love for the Slave and a determination—a *will* that justice, strong and unyielding, shall be done, where he has got a right to act; and you can form your own conclusion." When handling a question raising issues of "justice—right—Liberty the government and Constitution—Union—humanity, then . . . no man can move him."[39] Joseph Gillespie deemed his friend's "love of justice & fair play . . . his predominating trait . . . [It] was intensely strong. It was to this mainly that his hatred of slavery may be attributed." Lincoln "was wonderfully kind, careful & just. . . . He would rather disoblige a friend than do an act of injustice to a political opponent. . . . He was extremely just and fair minded He was gentle as a girl and yet as firm for the right as adamant." Judge David Davis was in no doubt that "Justice was Lincolns leading characteristic, modified by mercy—when possible. . . . When he formed his opinions he was firm, Especially about questions of justice—principle—&c." In wartime, this feature fused with an increasing reflection on the ways of the Almighty, an interventionist Providence, and divine justice. Leonard Swett explained, "As he became involved in matters of the gravest importance, full of great responsibility and great doubt, a feeling of religious reverence, and belief in God—his justice and overruling power—increased upon him. He was full of natural religion. . . . He believed in the great laws of truth, the rigid discharge of duty, his accountability to God, the ultimate triumph of right, and the overthrow of wrong."[40]

Lincoln's celebrated empathy and tolerant understanding of those who differed from him were stretched to breaking point by what he deemed the injustice of southern proslavery theologians and the doctrines that their northern Democrat sympathizers parroted. He scorned the Presbyterian Frederick A. Ross for concluding that "it is better for *some* people to be slaves; and, in such cases, it is the Will of God that they be such." The fact that determining God's will was to be left to Dr. Ross, who "sits in the shade, with gloves on his hands, and subsists on the bread that Sambo is earning in the burning sun," gave little confidence that he would "be actuated by that perfect impartiality, which has ever been considered most favorable to correct decisions."[41] This driest of dry wit gave way to something blunter when, in 1864, a Tennessee woman pestered the president for the release of her Confederate husband from a prisoner-of-war camp in Ohio, making much of her spouse's piety. Lincoln granted her request, but in doing so delivered a "political sermon" that he got Noah Brooks to publish in the *Washington Chronicle* under the headline (which he himself supplied) of "The President's Last, Shortest, and Best Speech": "You say your husband is a religious man; tell him . . . that . . . I am not much of a judge of religion, but that, in my opinion, the religion that sets men to rebel and fight against their government, because, as they think, that government does not sufficiently help some men to eat their bread on the sweat of other men's faces, is not the sort of religion upon which people can get to heaven!"[42]

If a sharp sense of the injustice of slavery shaped Lincoln's response to Nasby, so too—albeit with greater complexity—did the injustice of color prejudice. Racial egalitarians were rare among white people of his era, although a significant minority of Republicans—of whom Locke was one—worked openly before the war to advocate the rights of free black inhabitants of the United States. Lincoln himself was not one of this group: rather, he supported those conservative reformers who saw a route to emancipation in the voluntary emigration of free black Americans to colonies abroad. We can only speculate about how Lincoln read Locke's extravagant and pointed use of the word *nigger*. In private, Lincoln used the term (along with *cuffee*) in jokes and anecdotes. Yet he knew its offensive quality. He rarely used it in his letters or other texts, official or unofficial: when he did so he wrapped it in quotation marks as a form of disinfectant. If newspaper reports can be trusted, then the word featured in a few of his speeches during the 1850s, but only very occasionally and never as a term of deliberate disparagement.[43]

Having heard Lincoln speak at Columbus, Ohio, in September 1859, Locke was evidently startled by the politician's defensive and ungenerous statements about race; he thought it "curious" that the speaker denied supporting black suffrage and "took pains to go out of his way to affirm his support of the law of Illinois forbidding the intermarriage of whites and negroes."[44] Both context and substance of his speech, however, reveal why Lincoln would later warm to Locke's withering assault on the racial inhumanity of Nasbyites—those who played upon, and were consumed by, fear of black people. The very morning of Lincoln's address the *Ohio Statesman*, the state capital's Democratic newspaper, claimed he had supported the "vile conception" of black suffrage during the 1858 senatorial campaign. Lincoln began by quoting passages from his joint debates with Douglas including the disclaimer that he had "no purpose to introduce political and social equality between the white and black races." His rebuttal done, he turned to his main purpose: to show the "insidious," essentially proslavery, character of Douglas's doctrine of popular sovereignty and its betrayal of the nation's founding principles. In a stern conclusion, Lincoln returned to the issue of race, but now—in sharp contrast to its opening section—scolded Democrats whose fear of being called "negro worshippers" charted their politics. He made inclusive claims for black people; insisted that the Declaration of Independence embraced both white and black when it spoke of the equality of "all men"; and protested against the "popular sovereigns" who taught that "the negro is no longer a man but a brute." This was an allusion to Douglas's recent declaration "*As* the negro is to the crocodile, *so* the white man is to the negro." Lincoln's Columbus speech was the first of several during 1859 and 1860 where, outraged at this crass cascade of disdain, he rebuked Douglas for "teaching that the negro . . . ranks with the crocodile and the reptile," a formula that sought to "brutalize the negro" and legitimize slavery. Lincoln's unequivocal words made clear the chasm between his own racial ideas and those of the Little Giant.[45]

After Lincoln had spoken, Locke privately asked him about the value of his stand against black voting and racial intermarriage. Lincoln implied it was tactical: "The law means nothing. I shall never marry a negress, but I have no objection to anyone else doing so. If a white man wants to marry a negro woman, let him do it—*if the negro woman can stand it*." Lincoln knew how much it paid northern Democrats to portray Republicans as racial amalgamationists. Locke acknowledged these constraints and admired in Lincoln a good man of exceptional political honesty.[46]

Dispassionate historians recognize what Locke could not know in the late 1850s, that Lincoln was set on an evolutionary course that would see him sign an emancipation edict freeing most of the country's black slaves, press for a constitutional amendment to end slavery, and entertain an embryonic program of black rights and citizenship. It was a course that gave a keener edge to his reading of Nasby and encourages the proposition that in a small way Locke assisted in his radicalization. The president relished no piece more than "On Negro Emigration"—the quintessence of the pastor's ranting on race, which he could quote from memory—and was capable of his own dry humor at the expense of negrophobes.[47] A certain John McMahon of Towanda, Pennsylvania, sent a telegram to the president to educate him in "what is justice & what is truth to all men." Lincoln, he wrote, should respect the proposition: "Equal Rights & Justice to all white men in the United States forever. White men is in class number one & black men is in class number two & must be governed by white men forever." Lincoln drafted a reply purporting to be composed by his secretary; he kept a straight face as he explained that the president wanted to know "whether you are either a white man or black one, because in either case, you can not be regarded as an entirely impartial judge—It may be that you belong to a third or fourth class of *yellow* or *red* men, in which case the impartiality of your judgment would be more apparant."[48] It is clear, then, that Lincoln's delight in the egregious Nasby was far more than the relish of a joke. It was the double joy of recognizing a brilliant assault on ugly racial stereotyping, too. Nasby may have been wickedly funny, but he was also a scoundrel—and morally wicked with it.

* * *

Edwin Stanton had a superficial grasp of what Nasby was and what he meant to Lincoln. The humor of Nasby was not, as the secretary of war described it, "the God damned trash of a silly mountebank." Rather, Locke's creation was the weapon—as much broadsword as stiletto—that punctured the dubious morality of Copperheadism. Lincoln's appreciation of Nasby—as is true of all effective satire—had a moral dimension. If, as Leonard Swett maintained, Lincoln really did read Nasby "as much as he did the Bible," then their twin appeal lay in their working toward a common truth by radically different routes. That Lincoln turned to the pastor of "the Church uv the Noo Dispensashun" on what would be the final afternoon of his life, delaying dinner by reading Nasby aloud to his old friends Illinois governor Richard J. Oglesby and adjutant general Isham Nicholas Haynie of Springfield has its own poignancy.[49] Lincoln's last hours are more commonly remembered by his fateful visit to Ford's Theatre to watch a frivolous Victorian comedy, *Our American Cousin.* The more fitting marker of that time, and one better to remember him by, because it better represents his fundamental moral seriousness, was his continuing engagement with the ethical monstrosities of Petroleum Vesuvius Nasby.

CHAPTER FOUR

PURPOSE, FUNCTIONS, EFFECTS

Lincoln's irrepressible sense of humor was so central to his being, so frequently deployed in private exchanges and public settings, and so much a subject of comment by others that it naturally prompts the question, what was its purpose? What do Lincoln's compulsive joking and storytelling, his delight in the company of other raconteurs, and his immersion in the humorous writings of others reveal about the man himself and the succor he took from laughter? In part, his joking provided a means of empowerment—of imposing himself on others—but it also acted as a health-giving salve. Put simply, Lincoln's appetite for humor and his notorious vulnerability to depression were two sides of the same coin: laughter was a therapeutic antidote to the grievous low spirits to which he was prone. It is equally evident that in laughter the wartime president secured temporary respite from the rigors of national command.

Beyond this personal need, there is a broader question: what political and public role did Lincoln's humor play? Here the picture is complicated, not least because purpose and function—intent and effect—were not necessarily one and the same. Lincoln used humor with deliberation and precision to shape his conversations in public and private, deploying it to secure particular outcomes; in this respect his levity has commonly been regarded as a productive instrument and source of strength. But there were unintended consequences, too, for in the hands of his opponents Lincoln's reputation as a humorist functioned as a weapon that could be turned against him. Humor could be a double-edged sword.

Empowerment, Diversion, and Therapy

From an early age, Lincoln's command of comic storytelling and mimicry made him welcome and entertaining company. His odd, lanky appearance and bookish appetites might, in another young man, have been a recipe for social reticence and shyness. But, as would be true throughout his life, his physical awkwardness seems not to have troubled him unduly, if at all. Rather, he had a strong sense of self-worth and enjoyed the personal regard he won for his amiable wit and quaint stories. It is no secret that eliciting laughter generates and sustains a sense of power and authority in the teller. He understood that a fund of genial humor, effectively deployed, provided the means of commanding an audience and exerting influence. He discovered that here was a form of social empowerment that opened doors. We have already seen examples: how it helped, inter alia, to secure his election as a military captain in the Black Hawk War, win him the respect of fellow congressmen in his Washington boardinghouse, and make him the magnet for the smiling attention of lawyers and residents gathered at the county seats of the Eighth Circuit. Henry Villard, attending Lincoln's daily "levees" in the Illinois statehouse as president-elect, reported that their "most remarkable and attractive feature . . . was his constant indulgence of his story-telling propensity. Of course, all the visitors had heard of it and were eager for . . . a practical illustration of his pre-eminence in that line. He knew this, and took special delight in meeting their wishes."[1]

The "special delight" that Villard detected points to Lincoln's ease as a performer. He welcomed—relished, indeed—the role of entertainer and was invigorated by it. During his debates with Douglas in 1858 he seemed to grow stronger in mind and body over the course of the campaign, in contrast to his opponent, whose physical decline was striking. Lincoln did not possess the stage actor's ease of movement: contemporaries described his "awkward gesticulation, the contortions of countenance, and the stooping forward almost to the ground to enforce some . . . argument or . . . invective."[2] But with his gift for holding an audience's attention, whether on the political platform or at informal gatherings, he revealed aspects of the actor's craft and something of the actor's ego. Unusually tall, he had the confidence to attract further attention to his proportions by donning a stovepipe hat that elongated him almost to (if not beyond) the point of absurdity. His love of the theater expressed a sympathy with the inner stirrings and skills of the performer. Considering Shakespeare's tragedies to be "best read at home," he took great pleasure in farce and comedy in stage performance, and analyzing how it worked.[3] His own gift for comic performance—knowing how to squeeze the most humor out of his material and leading his audience to the climax of a story—made him a shrewd critic. Particularly fond of James Hackett's rendition of Falstaff, he had the confidence to advise the experienced actor on how to deliver a line so as to prompt the laugh that was waiting to be had.

There was, however, a troubled side to Lincoln's recourse to the comic. Like many humorists before and since, he was subject to dark moods—"blue spells"—that teetered on the edge of disabling depression. Jokes and anecdotes acted as therapy. His colleagues and acquaintances recognized their palliative function. Joshua F. Speed believed that telling anecdotes "was . . . necessary to [Lincoln's] . . . very existence": he didn't resort "to the bottle, to cards or dice—He had no fondness for any of these—Hence he sought relaxation in anecdotes." A law student in the Lincoln and Herndon office, noting the mutuality of gloom and merriment in Lincoln's makeup, learnt that "a very slight thing would break up his brooding."[4] A Springfield friend, hearing his distinctive guffaw, called the laughter "the President's life-preserver." Charles A. Dana recognized "that it was by the relief which . . . jests afforded to the strain of mind under which Lincoln had so long been living and to the natural gloom of a melancholy and desponding temperament . . . that the safety and sanity of his intelligence was maintained and preserved."[5] John Hay recorded a midnight visit of the president dressed in his nightshirt, clutching a volume of Thomas Hood's works, and—despite the oppressive anxieties of the day—seeking out his secretaries "that we may share with him the fun."[6]

No one better described the mercurial complexity of Lincoln's moods than Charles Adolphe Pineton, the Marquis de Chambrun, who accompanied Lincoln on his journey to City Point and Petersburg in late March 1865. "After a moment's inspection Mr. Lincoln left with you a sort of impression of vague and deep sadness. It is not too much to say that it was rare to converse with him a while without feeling something poignant," he wrote. Yet, strangely, "Mr. Lincoln was quite humorous, although one could always detect a bit of irony in his humor. . . . He willingly laughed either at what was said to him, or at what he said himself. But all of a sudden he would retire within himself; then he would close his eyes, and all his features would at once bespeak a kind of sadness as indescribable as it was deep." Eventually, "as though it were by an effort of his will, he would shake off this mysterious weight under which he seemed bowed; his generous and open disposition would again reappear. In one evening I happened to count over twenty of these alternations and contrasts."[7]

Lincoln himself explained: "If it were not for these stories, jokes, jests I should die; they give vent—are the vents—of my moods and gloom."[8] Defending his taste for bawdiness, he explained how "a real smutty story if it has the element of genuine wit in its composition, as most of such stories have, has the same effect on me that I think a good square drink of whisky has to an old toper. It puts new life into me. The fact is, I have always believed that a good laugh was good for both the mental and physical digestion." Jonathan Browning, gunsmith and transplanted Kentuckian, provided a graphic example of that physical tonic. He told how he and Lincoln swapped yarns when they met at his Quincy home as young men. They shared frontier southern backgrounds and an appetite for homespun humor. Lincoln chuckled when Browning told him he had got his first Bible by trading a gun for it. Quoting the prophet Isaiah, Lincoln quipped that the gunsmith had turned swords into plowshares. Browning then confessed that the traded gun had been defective with a "pretty weak" mainspring. In mock indignation Lincoln assumed "an exaggerated courtroom manner": "You mean that you cheated in a trade for a Bible—a Bible!" "Not exactly," Browning retorted. "When I got to looking through that Bible at home, I found about half the New Testament was missing." The uncontrolled mirth of the two men, in Browning's words, "near to shook the logs" of the cabin.[9] Years later, as president, Lincoln rarely knew such unrestrained and untroubled merriment, but he still sought peculiar comfort from laughing along with those who shared his sense of humor, notably William Seward and John Hay.

The sound of laughter was a magnet. General Joseph Kirkland recollected a visit to the White House when Lincoln, hearing merriment from his secretaries' room, put his head round the door and said, "I thought you were laughing pretty loud in here and that I should like to come in and laugh too."[10] The prospect of laughter drew him, too; hence the lure of the theater, where he was unabashed that people commented on his very audible "coarse laugh." He told Josiah Grinnell that he was especially "convulsed" by Falstaff's indignant response when Prince Hal protested that he himself, not the fat knight, had slain Hotspur: "Lord, how this world is given to lying." "We had some good war news yesterday and I was glad to unbend and laugh," Lincoln explained. "The acting was good and true to the case, according to my experiences, for each fellow tells his own story and smirches his rival."[11] Lincoln once remarked that "it was a common notion that those who laughed heartily and often never amounted to much—never made great men," but he never let this inhibit him. Indeed, his "undisguised and hearty" laugh was likened to a neighing horse.[12]

Lincoln was evangelistic about the reviving power of laughter. At the landmark cabinet meeting of September 22, 1862, where he unveiled the preliminary emancipation proclamation, the president began by reading out a short piece by Artemus Ward (the humorist Charles Farrar Browne), in which Ward, a preposterous itinerant circus showman, describes a customer's assault on Judas Iscariot in his wax exhibition of the Last Supper (which "kaved in Judasses hed"). "Gentlemen, why don't you laugh?" Lincoln asked his irritated colleagues. "With the fearful strain that is upon me night and day, if I did not laugh I should die."[13] Some months later Gideon Welles recorded Lincoln's surprise when Montgomery Meigs confessed not knowing about Robert Henry Newell's creation, Orpheus C. Kerr: "Why, have you not read those papers? . . . anyone who has not read them must be a heathen." That they lampooned an incompetent administration and belittled him personally did not stop him learning passages by heart. Turning to the secretary of the navy, the president chuckled: "Now the hits that are given to you, Mr. Welles I can enjoy, but I dare say they may have disgusted you while I was laughing at them. So vice versa as regards myself."[14] Of an unspecified member of the cabinet, he said—quoting Sydney Smith, a fellow depressive—that it would take a surgical operation to get a joke into his head.[15] He was probably referring to Chase, or perhaps Stanton. He could equally have said it about Sumner, whom he respected despite, not because of, the senator's limited sense of humor. By contrast, he cast himself as the grave digger in *Hamlet*, "for am I not noted as a fellow of infinite jest and humor, and is not my present life typical of that vocation?"[16]

Worthy of note, too, for its place in assisting his well-being, was Lincoln's particular relish of "anything that savored of the wit and humor of the soldiers." Much of their jesting was of the darkest kind, prompted by severe hardship, proximity to death, and appalling wounds. According to Noah Brooks, "any incident that showed that 'the boys' were mirthful and jolly in all their privations seemed to commend itself" to the president. He repeated the story of a soldier "carried to the rear of battle with both legs shot off, who, seeing a pie-woman hovering about, asked, 'Say old lady, are them pies sewed or pegged?'" He told of the soldier at Chancellorsville whose treasured crockery mug was shattered by a stray bullet as he was drinking coffee, leaving only its handle on his finger: "Johnny, you can't do that again!" he growled in the direction of the rebels.[17] The lesson of these tales, Lincoln believed, was that "neither death nor danger could quench the grim humor of the American soldier." It was not the cruelty of the troops' humor that appealed to him but the comforting evidence that both the president and his men shared in a common suffering, and together found a salve in grim jests.

Utility

Late in life, Lincoln would repeat with appreciative glee the description of a type of southwestern political orator who "mounted the rostrum, threw back his head, shined his eyes, opened his mouth, and left the consequences to God."[18] In sharp contrast, there was little in Lincoln's own speeches that was not planned and well calculated; when called on to speak impromptu, he tried to avoid saying anything of substance. Equally, his use of humor and stories in his public addresses and private conversations was rarely lacking in broader intent, and never designed to cover up empty thought. He applied humor with purpose and for advantage. Its utility can be categorized under six broad headings. At times it lay in crushing opponents. More commonly and cunningly, when used as a means of emphasizing his common touch—and even more when deployed as self-deprecation—humor could be a weapon of subtle attack. On other occasions it was a way of disingenuously planting a self-serving idea into the mind of his hearers. It provided, too, a means of tactical diversion or obfuscation; and it also had a role in relation to public morale. Above all, however, he used his stories as parables, as a pointed, accessible, and persuasive form of political explanation.

* * *

As an aspiring young politician Lincoln occasionally resorted to cruel and aggressive humor not simply to put his opponents on the defensive but to eviscerate, crush, and humiliate them. The roasting of Forquer and the "skinning" of Thomas, discussed earlier, were just two—if the most notorious—instances. Over time, however, Lincoln learnt to be more deft and subtle in sharpening a debating edge. As a maturing politician, drawing on his experience as a trial lawyer, he used gentler wit to put his opponents on the back foot while at the same time winning over his audience through genial good humor. No one was more aware of this maneuver than his chief adversary during the 1850s, Stephen Douglas. Lincoln began his determined reengagement with politics—prompted by the senator's dramatic repeal of the Missouri Compromise—in Springfield in October 1854. The Little Giant had declared, in heavy tones calculated to impress, "I will tell you what was the origin of the Nebraska bill. It was this, Sir! God created man, and placed before him both good and evil, and left him free to choose for himself. That was the origin of the Nebraska bill." Lincoln, according to the reporters, "looked the picture of good nature and patience," and replied with a smile, "I think it is a great honor to Judge Douglas that he *was the first man to discover that fact.*"[19] The audience's laughter not only discomfited Douglas but heralded ordeals to come, several of them during their joint debates in 1858. Aware that the crowd at one of these jousts had been profoundly impressed by his opponent's opening speech, Lincoln took his time before stirring. Apparently in deep thought, "he began very deliberately to rise" and in leisurely fashion took off his linen duster. As he handed it to one of the men behind him, he remarked, "Here, hold my coat while I stone Stephen!" The remark broke the tension for an audience well versed in the scriptures and the grim circumstances of that apostle's martyrdom. According to one of Lincoln's neighbors, "a roar of laughter . . . was followed by cheers. . . . Whether the remark was from a pure impulse of humor or was a well-calculated stroke of policy may not be known."[20]

A reporter for the politically friendly *New York Tribune* described Lincoln during these debates as "colloquial, affable, good-natured, almost jolly"—a view shared by Democratic observers. The newspaperman overstated his case, however, when he claimed, "His opponents are almost persuaded he is no opponent at all."[21] A Douglas Democrat, Albert Blair of Pike County, who attended the debate at Quincy, was not alone in his concern: "The manner in which . . . [Lincoln] would tax 'my friend Judge Douglas,' with a troublesome question, or answer him humorously with 'that reminds me of a story,' or with some other form of telling repartee, all resulting in tremendous laughter and applause, however it may have affected Mr. Douglas certainly worried me very much."[22] In fact, his hero was worried, too. Although the Little Giant declared that there "had not been a moment" when he feared Lincoln in debating matters of substance, and felt that he had held his own with the crowd just as well as his opponent, he confessed, "There is one thing, however, of which I stand constantly in dread. When Lincoln begins to tell a story I begin to get apprehensive. Every one of his stories seems like a whack upon my back—that is exactly the effect that the allegories and anecdotes, of which he is master, have upon me. Nothing else

. . . disturbs me. But when he begins to tell a story, I feel that I am to be overmatched."[23]

* * *

In his face-to-face engagement with the public—whether in the courtroom, on the political platform, at the White House, or elsewhere—Lincoln's recourse to stories and jokes was designed to remind his hearers that he was a westerner of lowly origins who knew the backwoods and the prairie at first hand. Through his particular brand of humor, delivered in his peculiar Kentucky-Indiana accent and in language that had "the smack of the soil" (as Harriet Beecher Stowe put it), he wanted the common people to see that he was one of them: a natural man lacking artifice, able to engage with ordinary farmers and laborers on equal terms. The journalist Ben Perley Poore described how the president "will sometimes throw his legs upon the table, as if in his law office in Springfield, and illustrate his position by a good story, or by a colloquial expression, drawn from the mother wit and humor of the prairie people. But this pleasant manner endears him the more to the great mass of those who elected him."[24]

Lincoln's lifelong self-identification with plain folk was closely allied to his chronic habit of self-deprecation and self-mockery. This kind of humor amounted to far more than a means of securing a laugh by preempting comments about his strange looks, modest upbringing, and calculated eccentricities. When shrewdly used, it was also a means of advantage, by enlisting the audience on the side of the underdog. It was a debating ploy that one historian has dubbed Lincoln's "big man–little man" technique, one which he used throughout his pre-presidential years against not only Forquer, Thomas, and Cartwright but also some of the biggest oratorical beasts in the Illinois Democracy. One of these was Usher F. Linder, with whom he engaged in the legislature on the question of the state bank in 1837, with a speech—the first of his to be published verbatim—that cast "the gentleman from Coles as decidedly my superior" and the speaker himself as "*small game.*" Linder's preeminence conceded, Lincoln then turned the concession against its subject: "In one faculty, at least, there can be no dispute of the gentleman's superiority over me, and most other men; and that is, the faculty of entangling a subject, so that neither himself, or any other man, can find head or tail to it." Later in the speech Lincoln described Linder's move to have the state bank investigated as "exclusively the work of politicians; a set of men who have interests aside from the interests of the people, and who, to say the most of them, are, taken as a mass, at least one long step removed from honest men." Then he added, with winning self-disparagement, "I say this with the greater freedom because, being a politician myself, none can regard it as personal."[25]

Lincoln used a similar technique in his political wrestling with Douglas throughout the 1850s, taking on the identity of a modest provincial facing the "world wide renown" of the Democrats' prime hope for the White House. His opponent enjoyed the status of "a very *great man*," while he himself was "only a small man"—the heavy irony of this language intensified by the sight of the diminutive Little Giant standing next to the elongated Lincoln. His own insignificance ("nobody has ever expected me to be President") made him a mere dog compared with the leonine Douglas. The modesty was, of course, false, and the audiences knew it—not least because Lincoln, practiced wrestler that he was, knew how to turn his opponent's force against him. "Douglas is a great man—at keeping from answering questions he don't want to answer," he jested in 1856. Most memorably, in his House Divided speech of June 1858, he quoted Ecclesiastes: "a *living dog* is better than a *dead lion*," adding, "Judge Douglas, if not a *dead* lion *for this work* [of resisting the spread of slavery], is at least a *caged* and *toothless* one."[26]

Even as president, this habit of self-deprecation had its uses, notably in dealing with a dilemma or taking the sting out of a conversation. When Owen Lovejoy and a western delegation secured Lincoln's agreement to an exchange of soldiers between the eastern and western theaters, the secretary of war flatly refused to implement the scheme, telling Lovejoy that the president was "a damned fool" for ordering it. Bewildered, the Illinois congressman returned to tell Lincoln, who paused before saying, "If Stanton said I was a damned fool, then I must be one, for he is nearly always right, and generally says what he means. I will step over and see him."[27]

* * *

Lincoln also found in laughter and humor a means of—sometimes disingenuously—planting a self-serving idea. The national newspapermen who descended on Illinois during 1858 to cover the joint debates included Henry Villard of New York. Sheltering together one evening during a thunderstorm, Lincoln told the young reporter "that, when he was clerking in a country store, his highest ambition was to be a member of the State Legislature." He continued, with a chuckle: "Since then, of course, I have grown some, but my friends got me into THIS. I did not consider myself qualified for the United States Senate. . . . Now, to be sure . . . I am convinced that I am good enough for it; but, in spite of it all, I am saying to myself every day: 'It is too big a thing for you; you will never get it.' Mary insists, however, that I am going to be Senator and President of the United States, too." These words he followed with a roar of laughter, with his arms around his knees, and shaking all over with mirth at his wife's ambition. "Just think," he exclaimed, "of such a sucker as me as President!"[28] Lincoln laughed, but his intent was utterly serious. Observing the etiquette of modesty with his rollicking laughter, he cunningly dropped into an eastern reporter's mind the idea that he could be run for the presidency.

As a lawyer, too, Lincoln wielded seemingly innocuous, random humor to plant a seed that would later shape the deliberations of a jury. During a lunch break, it is said, he told jurors the story of a small boy who ran to summon his father. "Paw, come quick," he panted. "The hired man and Sis are up in the haymow, and he's a-pullin' down his pants and she's a-liftin' up her skirts and Paw they're gettin' ready to pee all over our hay!" The father replied, "Son, you've got your facts absolutely right, but you've drawn a completely wrong conclusion." Later, in court, following his opponent's lengthy winding-up speech, Lincoln told the jurors, "My learned opponent has his facts absolutely right, but has drawn completely wrong conclusions." Lincoln won the case.[29] In a separate trial, the opposing counsel unsuccessfully entered a challenge against the selection of a particular juror, on the grounds that the man was acquainted with Lincoln. When it was

Lincoln's turn to examine the panel, he too inquired if any of them knew his opponent. The judge reprimanded him for wasting the court's time: "The mere fact that a juror knows your opponent does not disqualify him." "No, your Honor," Lincoln replied, "but I am afraid some of the gentlemen may not know him, which would place me at a disadvantage."[30] His dry humor was designed to color the jury's subsequent view of the opposing lawyer's pleading.

* * *

Humor also provided a means of diversion. One of Lincoln's associates judged that in the courtroom he mostly resorted to stories to shore up a faltering case: he "never indulged in fun when he had a great case—one which he believed was right—. . . but if his case were weak he would tell stories, cover his opponent, the witness etc with ridicule, keep court & jury shrieking with laughter, but when he was *sure*, he was grave."[31] In the political sphere he learnt to use anecdotes as a way of turning, redirecting, deflecting, or smoothing a conversation without giving offence. He recognized that "the sharpness of a refusal or the edge of a rebuke may be blunted by an appropriate story, so as to save wounded feeling and yet serve the purpose."[32] John Hay told how in late 1863 "an infernal nuisance" of a Brooklyn postmaster, with his eyes on the following year's presidential election, "fastened himself to the Tycoon . . . and tried to get into conversation on the subject of the succession." Lincoln "quickly put him off with a story of his friend Jesse Dubois," who as state auditor controlled the use of the Illinois statehouse in Springfield. "An itinerant quack preacher" requested it as the venue for a religious lecture. "'What's it about' said Jesse. 'The Second Coming of Christ' said the parson. 'Nonsense' roared Uncle Jesse, 'if Christ had been to Springfield once, and got away, he'd be damned clear of coming again.'"[33]

One of the president's most stressful tasks as leader of the new administration in 1861 was dealing with the avalanche of applicants for government posts. He was bombarded with far more requests than he had jobs. One day a delegation called to urge the appointment of an acquaintance as commissioner to the Sandwich Islands. They earnestly emphasized not only his fitness for the post but also his poor health, which would benefit from the balmy climate. The president closed the interview with affected regret: "Gentlemen, I am sorry to say that there are eight other applicants for that place, and they are all sicker than your man."[34] To another office seeker, also disappointed, the president said, "I had in my pig sty a little bit of a pig, that made a terrible commotion—do you know why? Because the old sow had just one more little pig than she had teats, and the little porker that got no teat made a terrible squealing."[35]

Humor helped deflect protests about conscription. In what may have been an apocryphal tale, Lincoln met a deputation from an Illinois village who complained about the draft. As "the Aesop of the new world," he eased their concerns with the story of a "little one horse village in Maryland, whose quota . . . was one man." The enrolling officer solemnly demanded from the old woman at one of the farmhouses "the name of every male creature" there. She listed them all, including a certain Billy Bray, on whom the lot fell in the draft. When the provost marshal came for his conscript, he discovered that Mr. Bray was the farmer's donkey. "So," said Lincoln to his fellow Illinoisans, "gentlemen you may be the donkey of your town and escape. Therefore don't distress yourselves by meeting trouble half way."[36]

* * *

Lincoln used comic storytelling to present a mien of serenity, even when deeply troubled. He understood that one of his responsibilities was to help lift the gloom in the face of Union setbacks and thus sustain morale. Receiving a visitor at the White House in July 1862 soon after the rearguard action at Malvern Hill, Lincoln remarked on the man's very sad face, which he said reminded him of a story. The visitor retorted that "this situation is too grave for the telling of anecdotes." The president is said to have replied with irritation, "Senator, do you think that this situation weighs more heavily upon you than it does upon me? If the cause goes against us, not only will the country be lost, but I shall be disgraced to all time. But what would happen if I appeared upon the streets of Washington to-day with such a countenance as yours? The news would spread throughout the country that the President's very demeanor is an admission that defeat is inevitable. And I say to you, sir, that it would be better for you to infuse some cheerfulness into that countenance of yours as you go about upon the streets of Washington."[37]

It was not easy to maintain a demeanor of buoyant good humor: Lincoln was often caught looking dejected in public. But he made conscious efforts to lighten the mood. When a delegation of anxious bank presidents called at the White House during a particularly gloomy period of the war, Lincoln wanted to encourage their confidence in the future and show he was not downcast. He was reminded, he said, of a time when as a young man he boarded with a Presbyterian deacon. One night he heard a rap on his door: "Arise Abraham," the deacon insisted, "the day of judgment has come!" Lincoln leapt out of bed and rushed to the window to see a shower of stars. "But I looked beyond those falling stars," he said, "and far back in the heavens I saw—fixed, apparently, and immovable—the grand old constellations with which I was so well acquainted. No, gentlemen; the world did not come to an end then, nor will the Union now!"[38]

* * *

Above all else, however, Lincoln's stories served as a colorful means of instruction and elucidation. "He seemed never to talk without some definite aim in view," one acquaintance reflected. "The few stories I heard him relate were told in each instance to illustrate some well-defined point."[39] According to Noah Brooks, "His anecdotes were seldom told for the sake of the telling, but because they . . . shed a light on the argument that nothing else could." Lincoln himself told Chauncey Depew, "They say I tell a great many stories; I reckon I do, but I have found in the course of a long experience that common people, *common people*, take them as they run, are more easily influenced and informed through the medium of broad illustration than in any other way."[40]

As president, he was irritated by those who saw him as a simple entertainer with a reservoir of jokes. At the Soldiers' Home in June 1863 a group of late evening visitors found him preparing for bed, his face lined with anxiety and weariness. "The drooping eyelids, looking almost swollen; the dark bags beneath the eyes; the deep marks about the large and expressive mouth; the flaccid muscles of the jaws, were all so majestically pitiful" that one of the callers, Silas W. Burt, felt keenly the presumptuous invasion of his peace. As they were leaving, an inebriated army officer "slapped the President on his knee and said, 'Mr. President, tell us one of your good stories.'" Lincoln "drew himself up, and turning his back as far as possible upon the Major, with great dignity addressed the rest of us, saying, 'I believe I have the popular reputation of being a story-teller, but I do not deserve the name in its general sense; for it is not the story itself, but its purpose or effect, that interests me. I often avoid a long and useless discussion by others or a laborious explanation on my own part by a short story that illustrates my point of view. . . . No, I am not simply a story-teller.'"[41] Elsewhere, when accosted by a visitor who said he called simply to hear a story, Lincoln asked where he lived. "Western New York," he replied. "Well," said the president, "that's a good enough country without stories."[42]

In the courtroom, Lincoln used apposite tales to win the confidence of juries composed of commonsensical plain men lacking in formal education. Exposing the false logic of an opposing counsel, he said he was reminded of "the cooper who, having trouble in closing up a barrel, put a boy inside to hold the head in place. The plan worked so well that the cooper drove on the hoops and finished the job, forgetting all about the boy or how he was to be gotten out." In another case, defending a farmer whose hogs had damaged a neighbor's crops, he fixed the jury's attention on the condition of the plaintiff's fence—and then held them rapt with the ludicrous story of a hog that grew increasingly confused by a fence so crooked that, after each attempt to break through, it found itself back where it started.[43]

Stories and striking images gave Lincoln the means of driving home political arguments with engaging economy. When John Pope telegraphed Washington that he had captured five thousand of Beauregard's men, was marching on the Confederates, and on the morrow would have the rebels in his power, the cabinet asked the president for his opinion. "That reminds me," he replied, of an "old woman in Sangamon Co. who was ill." The doctor came and prescribed some medicine for her constipation. Returning the next morning, he found her "fresh & well getting breakfast." Asked if the medicine had worked, she confirmed that it had. "How many [bowel] movements?" he inquired. "142," she replied. "Madame I am serious," the physician replied, "I know you are joking. How many?" "142." "Madame, I *must* know," he insisted, "you couldn't have had 142. It is necessary I have the exact no. of movements." "I tell you 142," she said, "140 of them *wind*." The story told, Lincoln added simply, "I am afraid Pope's captures are 140 of them wind." That closed the discussion.[44]

Examples of Lincoln's humorous economy in argument are legion. He recognized that war with foreign powers had to be avoided at all costs ("one war at a time" was his precept). During the *Trent* crisis of late 1861, Orville Browning urged him not to yield to London's demands for the release of the Confederate envoys seized from a British ship: England was only bluffing and would not dare to fight. Lincoln reminded his friend of a vicious bulldog back in Springfield. Neighbors denied it was dangerous, but Lincoln recalled the words of a man who was not so sure: "I know the bulldog will not bite. You know he will not bite, but does the bulldog know he will not bite?"[45] Joseph Gillespie recollected discussing the theory of state sovereignty with Lincoln, who declared that "the advocates of that theory always reminded him of the fellow who contended that the proper place for the big kettle was inside of the little one." Facing objections to the declaration of martial law in Kentucky from a cabinet member who noted that in recent elections only a few qualified voters had been excluded from the polls, Lincoln cited the case of Sarah, an unmarried mother, whose plea in extenuation was that "the baby was a little one."[46]

Lincoln's versatility lay not just in finding a story for almost every occasion but also in applying the same tale in different contexts. He several times deployed the story of a barber faced with shaving a lantern-jawed customer with cheeks so hollow that the barber "couldn't get down into the valleys with the razor." Ingeniously, he determined "to stick his finger in the man's mouth and press out the cheeks." However, "he cut clean through the cheek and into his own finger. He pulled the finger out of the man's mouth and snapped the blood off it and looked at him and said: 'There, you lantern-jawed cus, you've made me cut my finger.'" General Horace Porter heard the president tell this to illustrate the dangers England faced in assisting the South: "In the end she will find she has only cut off her own finger."[47] On other occasions, Lincoln used the same anecdote to show that "we've got to be mighty cautious how we manage the negro question."[48]

The Irish teetotaler who wanted whisky added to his glass of lemonade "all unbeknownst to mesilf" offered Lincoln a means of signaling that in some particularly challenging circumstances, he was keen to turn a blind eye. So it was with General Thomas Ewing's proposal in August 1863 to deport thousands of Missouri civilians from guerilla-supporting communities and free their slaves. When Frank Blair visited Lincoln to seek his views, the president took refuge in the anecdote, leaving his meaning plain. Blair reported later to General Schofield, "The inference is that old Abe would be glad if you would dispose of the Guerrillas and would not be sorry to see the negroes set free, if it can be done without his being known in the affair as having instigated it. He will be certain to recognize it afterward as a military necessity."[49] With the Confederates' defeat imminent, he said he would be saved a deal of bother if his generals allowed Jefferson Davis to escape, "all unbeknownst" to himself.[50]

Other tales that Lincoln often deployed to dodge issues, or caution against addressing troubles that might never arise, included the farmer who "plowed around" the tree stump that blocked his way. This, Lincoln told Senator James Harlan, was how to handle the "Mormon question." He gave similar advice to General R. C. Schenk, whose work in recruiting African American troops in Maryland was complicated by the difficulty in distinguishing between free black men and runaway slaves. An equally graphic anecdote centered on a group of traveling Methodist ministers who were approaching a river in Illinois that—in Lincoln's words as recalled by George Templeton Strong—was "ugly to cross, ye know, because the waters was up. And they got considerin' and discussin' how they should git across it, and they talked about it for two hours, and one on 'em thought they had ought to cross one way when they got there, and another another way, and they got quarrelin' about it, till at last an old brother put in, and he says, says he, 'Brethren, this here talk ain't no use. I never cross a river until I come to it.'"[51] This, the president explained, was how he handled the pressure to take more radical measures relating to slavery.

The Genial President

Lincoln's supporters seized on his studied use of humor to show how an occupant of the White House could remain a genial man of the people. The Republican press had already made much of his reputation as a good-humored storyteller during the presidential campaign of 1860. On Election Day, the *New York Times* published the letter of a Springfield resident praising his neighbor's intellect, moderation, strong will, and sociability: "He enjoys a joke; tells a good story; is very kind and affable, and withal a most worthy gentleman."[52] As president-elect, holding court in the Illinois state capitol, "Old Abe" won plaudits for his simple manner and lack of affectation. An Indiana newspaperman deemed him "accessible enough to satisfy the most democratic constituency," and concluded, "One needs to be in his presence but a few minutes to be convinced that, notwithstanding the . . . critical position in which he is placed, he has lost nothing of his proverbial geniality of disposition, his buoyancy of spirits, or his love of dry humour, good jokes and droll stories."[53]

While the president faced up to the ordeal of wartime office—the setbacks in the field, and the high-risk decisions over emancipation, civil liberties, and other divisive policies—his supporters wove his "inveterate habit of telling ludicrous stories to illustrate his opinions" into a larger appreciation of his strength of moral character and determination. Expecting the administration to be badly bruised at the fall elections in 1862, some Republicans conceded that Lincoln's love of a joke was "a better thing in peace than in war" and that he was "neither wiser than Solomon nor abler than Michael." But, they asked, "what President have we had these many years who ever manifested more ability to cope with the gigantic questions that like an army of hydras surround the White House?"[54]

During the course of the war, proadministration newspapers grew increasingly keen to broadcast "the president's latest story." Those who provided this material included Lincoln's private secretary, John Hay, who cultivated a warm relationship with several journalists and supplied them with examples of the president's wit, as long as the stories passed the test of respectability. It was he who helped circulate Lincoln's tale, noted earlier, of the quack preacher who wanted to sermonize in Springfield on the Second Coming. Hay had urged that the story not be repeated, "being blasphemous & calculated to hurt the 'Quaker vote.'" He specifically charged his friend Charles Halpine not to use it, but Halpine—a staunch War Democrat—could not resist the temptation, though he did tone down the language of Hay's text.[55] In fact, Halpine mostly served the administration well, particularly after the antidraft riots in New York in July 1863, when he worked hard to build support for the war among the Irish. To that end he created an affectionately comic figure, Private Miles O'Reilly, a fervent loyalist whose political support for Lincoln and apparent familiarity with the White House led some readers to mistake fiction for fact. Hay's letters to Halpine ("My Dear Miles") provided his friend with the details that gave misleading authenticity to O'Reilly's meetings with the president. The tales reinforced the image of Lincoln as a man of warmth, humor, and humanity. The defining episode was the president's pardoning of O'Reilly, who languished in prison as punishment for his satirical poems about the Union's military command. This act of executive humanity prompted further doggerel from the grateful soldier:

> Long life to you Misther Lincoln!
> May you die both late an' aisy;
> An' whin you lie wid the top of aich toe
> Turned up to the roots of a daisy,
> May this be your epitaph, nately writ—
> "Though thraitors abused him vilely,
> He was honest an' kindly, he loved a joke,
> An' he pardoned Miles O'Reilly!"[56]

Appreciation of the power of Lincoln's humor to enforce his argument and logic—"both unseasonable at times and irresistible always"—played a significant role in characterizing the president as the representative American during his reelection year.[57] One commentator described his jokes as a "happy device" in prompting public understanding: "a joke goes for a joke, and not for solemn dogma; an illustration is accepted as such, and not necessarily as a leaf from history which one must swear to." Those distressed by them were "silly people" with "very feeble intellectual digestion." Hearing a presidential story designed to expose the folly of some proposition, "Mr Feeblemind . . . goes home, consults Plutarch and can't find it there; gets down his Bible, it isn't there; looks in the American Encyclopaedia, it is not there; so he is forced to the conclusion that the President told a wrong story, . . . can not see its truth, and doubts if the war can ever be ended till there is a change of Administrations."[58] The Bostonian women's rights activist and Garrisonian abolitionist Caroline Healey Dall rebuked those "fine ladies" of the Women's Loyal League who were repelled by the president's "homely manners" and jokes. "As a nation," she wrote, "we are an intelligent, but not a cultivated people. Mr. Lincoln fairly represents our average attainment, and he has never written a letter that the humble of his constituents cannot understand." He deserved prayers, not criticism: "Aesop told some stories, and his homely wisdom has kept his name alive. Our Divine Master knew little of classic lore or historic legend," but he did know how to tell a simple, instructive story.[59] For the New York lawyer T. J. Barnett, this was why "the people can understand him so well, and why the politicians can not comprehend him at all." The people's affectionate regard, he declared, was "absolutely filial" and savored "of the *household.*"[60]

This benign reading of Lincoln's humor was sufficiently powerful for commercial interests to exploit it in wartime compilations of jokes and stories, supposedly (but rarely) originating with the president. The publishers of *Old Abe's Joker, or Wit at the White House* asked "what could be more natural than to associate with 'quips and cranks and wanton wiles,' the name of one who so greatly enjoys and successfully perpetrates the fine old, full-flavored joke" (Figure 1; see gallery of images beginning on page 123). Graphic advertisements for *Old Abe's Jokes, Fresh from Abraham's Bosom* ("Comprising all his issues excepting the 'Green Backs'") showed the bearded rail-splitter president entertaining a rapt audience of smiling common folk.

It was in this spirit of appreciation that in February 1864 William Cullen Bryant's radical *New York Evening Post* offered a commentary on a wide array of Lincoln's jokes and "little stories." Since its intention was to show how these were the mark of a purposeful, genial, and wise commander in chief, the column was an early contribution to the presidential campaign. Bryant's purpose was to show how the tortured mind of a suffering, bone-weary, and patient president found occasional relief "in an appropriate anecdote or well turned jest." His "atrocious" puns brought him innocent delight. He found humor when bedridden with contagious varioloid ("I've got something now that I can give to everybody"). When charged by an unnamed member of Congress (Ben Wade, in fact) for diverting attention from serious matters by ludicrous allusions—"Mr. Lincoln, I think you would have your joke if you were within a mile of hell"—he replied, "Yes, that is about the distance to the Capitol." But, Bryant explained, in addition to their therapeutic value, stories and wit served as a means of rebuke to those who wasted his time with trivial requests. Beneath his levity lay a stratum of ethical rock.[61]

This understanding of the moral grounding of the president's humor inflected mainstream Union opinion. As voters turned out on the day of the election, November 8, Cyrus Wick, an infantryman of the 17th Indiana Regiment stationed near Nashville, distilled in admiring verse the essence of Father Abraham's appeal:

> The man who now has nations for beholders,
> Who dared to say his Government was made
> To lift the weights from off all men's shoulders,
> Though for a time its purpose was delayed;
> While Treason's banded millions were arrayed,
> Displayed the art that made those hosts afraid.
> Few would have thought who heard him telling stories,
> And jokes that rustic hearers might applaud,
> That he would be one of our country's glories,
> And live to send those edicts far abroad
> That made enslavers tremble and be awed.[62]

"The Smutty Joker"

In setting out the value and benefits of Lincoln's storytelling, his supporters were above all responding to those who exploited, and often distorted, the president's appetite for the comic. The history of his time in office was one of opponents' constant and increasing disdain for a chief magistrate whose taste in jokes, they sneered, made him unfit for his position. Democrats had already berated him for his "smutty jokes" during the senatorial campaign of 1858, and from the moment of his presidential nomination in May 1860 opposition presses ridiculed a candidate of whom nothing favorable could be said "except that he once drove oxen—went barefooted—split rails—is a passably good lawyer—tells a smutty story in good style—[and] is the ugliest man in the West."[63] The *New York Herald* invoked a reproachful "Old Whig" who sneered that Lincoln "had a great deal of rather low wit; was capital at vulgar repartee; and could tell more obscene anecdotes than any other man I ever knew."[64] A Democratic biographer declared, "When he laughs, people think they are at the entrance of the Mammoth Cave."[65] Observing the candidate in Springfield, the painter Alban Jasper Conant asked himself, "Is this the man I must vote for to guide the country in these feverish times—one who trifles with great personalities and issues and dismisses both with a joke?"[66]

During the crisis winter of 1860–61, the president-elect's determined jocularity provided much ammunition for those keen to deem him politically out of his depth. "The man has a terrible penchant for story-telling," a Connecticut newspaperman reported from Springfield. "He seemed *to forget,* at times, *his position* as President elect, in his reception room, and to feel that he was again 'on the circuit' in some country-seat . . . about the *bar-room fire,* whiling away the evening hours with amusing reminiscences and *ludicrous anecdotes.* I verily believe he would crack a joke at the crack of doom." His speeches en route to Washington likewise drew Democrats' scorn. One lamented, "When the people ask for bread he gives them a stone. He dispatches the most serious subjects with a joke, and asserts, with a smile, that the present crisis is purely 'artificial.'"[67]

Some of his own party, too, took exception to Lincoln's lack of dignity. A Rhode Island Republican sighed that it was "with unfeigned mortification I have read his jokes & the accounts of his kissing young women. Imagine Washington on a journey to the Federal Capital, joking, kissing women. When the Queen of England . . . expresses her solicitude for our welfare . . . , Mr. Lincoln sees no danger & is reported to have said 'No one is hurt,' and jokes, & kisses the women." *Harper's Weekly*, on the eve of his inauguration, presented "Our Presidential Merryman" holding a drained glass in his hand while "engaged in a lively exchange of wit and humor" with a set of rough, inebriated companions, as a funeral hearse marking the death of the Union passes by (Figure 2). He drily contemplated sacrificing Fort Sumter in return for Virginia's continuing loyalty: "a State for a fort is no bad business."[68] Once inaugurated, Lincoln held a reception for the members of the Peace Conference gathering in Washington. The Virginia Unionist William C. Rives thought the president "utterly unimpressed with the gravity of the crisis & the magnitude of his duties." He "seems to think of nothing but jokes & stories."[69]

Throughout the four years of the war both Confederates and critics in the Union seized on Lincoln's humor as a stick with which to beat him. With the war taking its early toll in the summer of 1861, an embittered Confederate sympathizer, Adalbert Volck, drew Lincoln as a jester in "The Comedy of Death," sharing the stage with an array of toy soldiers resembling the Union's high command[70] (Figure 3). Southern presses ridiculed "the obscene ape of Illinois," whose every policy—his emancipation scheme included—was "a little joke," whose inveterate jesting was evidence of "bad heart," and whose "grotesque and monstrous" levity exposed his desperation in "the hour of tribulation."[71] In reality, their attacks had little capacity to wound. Northern critics, however—whether from his own party or the opposition Democrats—did succeed in putting Lincoln loyalists on the defensive.

Their common charge was that the president's appetite for low jokes exposed a disabling lack of gravitas and principle. Within weeks of the first shot, some Presbyterian divines called on the president to urge a halt to the war, allegedly prompting this response: "Sir, peace with the South is as impossible as it is for you to sleep with my wife tonight." A shocked conservative despaired, "Here you have a specimen of the malignity and vulgarity of the brutal old fool."[72] Radicals, too, rebuked Lincoln for substituting wit and humor for principle. Abolitionists before the war had criticized him for believing that "wit, sharp repartee, readiness of speech, [and] good humor" could "compensate for moral cowardice, or ignorance of the first truths of liberty." Now, as president, he responded to demands for strong measures by taking refuge in storytelling. Jane Grey Swisshelm complained, "A Western Senator visited him on official business and reciprocated by telling an anecdote the President had not before heard. After he rose to leave Mr. Lincoln remarked: 'Wait a moment; I want you to give me the notes of that story!'" When the Quaker Anna E. Dickinson visited him to press for better enforcement of the Emancipation Proclamation, he began with a diversionary story that she boldly interrupted: "I didn't come to hear stories. I can read better ones in the papers any day than you can tell me."[73]

A related complaint was the charge that Lincoln used humor to mask, or compensate for, his deficiencies in strategy and command. Soldiers who encountered him at receptions or reviews were alarmed to discover their commander in chief painfully ignorant of military matters and "giggling & uttering poor coarse jokes" in a "very vulgar & undignified" manner; the chaplain of an Illinois regiment was upset "at such a time to see him exhibit himself, publickly, in so hilarious a way."[74] Following the failure of the 1862 Peninsula campaign, McClellan's removal, and his later reappointment, General John E. Wool privately dismissed the president as a smutty joker lacking "the first qualification to govern a great people."[75] A few weeks later, after the calamity at Fredericksburg, George Templeton Strong lamented, "A year ago we laughed at the Honest Old Abe's grotesque genial Western jocosities, but they nauseate us now"; he entertained the possible replacement of the president by Hamlin, who might "be a change for the better, none for the worse being conceivable."[76] Twelve months on, a despondent Salmon P. Chase dismissed him as "purposeless," judging him "Firm only from his inertia. . . . Has no practical power.

No cabinet meetings for two years for counsel. Meetings for jokes. . . . Must be a change at the White House."[77] Elizabeth Cady Stanton was equally trenchant: "I say Butler or Fremont or some man on their platform for the next President & let Abe finish up his jokes in Springfield."[78]

The complaints of disaffected Union loyalists—members of the cabinet, military officers, and ordinary soldiers and citizens—gave greater plausibility to the barbs of the antiadministration press. Samuel Medary's newspaper, the *Crisis,* deemed the president's habit of "replying to the most momentous questions and the gravest personages with a story and a joke" as even "more ominous and more appalling" than the "careless brutality" of a Nero.[79] Chauncey Burr's Copperhead journal, the *Old Guard,* forgave the commanders in the field for the failure of the Union armies, pinning the blame squarely on the president. "We have great confidence in Mr. Lincoln as a good story-teller, an excellent joker and first class buffoon; but no confidence in him whatever, as a military strategist." In an imaginary set of instructions from Lincoln to his provost marshals, a Democratic satirist included the order, "If you hear any man say that I know better how to tell stories, than how to conduct the affairs of the nation, he is disloyal—arrest him."[80]

The president's sense of humor also served—mostly in antiadministration broadsides—as a measure of his cruel disregard for the suffering victims of war. Lincoln the "heartless buffoon" became a recurrent theme. The opposition presses were quick to circulate the essence of a powerful *Harper's Weekly* cartoon, "Columbia Confronts Her Children," published shortly after the grievous Union losses at Fredericksburg. A female figure with her arm outstretched—Columbia—points at Lincoln, who stands outside the War Department between two figures, Edwin M. Stanton and Joseph Hooker, and asks "Where are my 15,000 sons, murdered at Fredericksburg?" Lincoln's callous answer, "This reminds me of a little joke . . . ," prompts an outraged interruption: "Go tell your joke at Springfield!!"[81] (Figure 4). Another cartoon cast him as "Manager Lincoln." Standing in front of a lowered curtain, the sole figure on an empty stage, he is an ingratiating, hand-wringing, but smiling impresario, with a pistol, sword, and the other debris of a routed army at his feet. "Ladies and Gentlemen," he announces, "I regret to say that the Tragedy, entitled The Army of the Potomac, has been withdrawn . . . and I have sub-stituted three new and striking Farces or Burlesques."[82]

When, a few months later, the president was reported to be in excellent spirits, a Democratic editor asked, "Does the pleasant speaker of parables divine some hideous joke in the condition of our na-tional affairs? President Lincoln's humor is proverbially curious. He was 'in excellent spirits' on the battle-field of Antietam with the mangled corpses of our dead soldiers around him—in such 'excel-lent spirits' that he would fain regale himself with the melody of a negro song."[83] Lincoln's visit to Gettysburg for the dedication of the national cemetery in November 1863 gave rise to a further portrayal of the commander in chief as an unfeeling butcher of men, in the company of an equally insensitive secretary of state: "With the groans of the wounded still resounding in the air—the corpses of the slain still unburied—the bereaved still clad in the emblems of mourning, and their tears still flowing—these men meet to laugh and joke and electioneer."[84] Lincoln had prompted "loud and vulgar and profane mirth among the tombs of those we . . . respected in life," when remarking, in response to a calls for a speech, that the only way he could avoid saying foolish things was to say nothing at all.[85] The president had indeed held his tongue on the eve of his address, aware that his impromptu dry wit had caused him embarrassment in the past, most recently on the journey to Gettysburg.[86]

A further, common accusation in the charge sheet against Lin-coln the irrepressible joker stood at odds with the other indictments. No longer the incapable buffoon unable to restrain his appetite for vulgar fun, he here became the fanatic who indulged a love of dark, sadistic, and quixotic humor through savage and dictatorial policies. These were cruel, unfunny jokes played by a tyrant who took amused pleasure in his disregard for the Constitution. Emancipation, the suspension of habeas corpus, the draft, black troops, reconstruc-tion, military rule, and the policies associated with the prosecution of a hard war were evidence of this warped sense of humor. When Lincoln proposed a scheme of compensated emancipation during the earlier phases of the war, a Louisville editor vented his disdain: "It is bad enough to have the negroes among us at all, but the idea of paying millions of dollars for the privilege, is a little too serious a joke."[87] Disgusted by the president's racial policies, Chauncey Burr sarcastically told him to

> crack your low jokes, Massa Lincoln—
> Only white men to ruin are hurled—
> So put your foot down, Massa Lincoln,
> And trample them out of the world.[88]

The Democratic *Wisconsin Patriot* routinely denigrated each of Lincoln's policies as expressions of his disturbed jocularity, whether disciplining a disloyal general by giving him command of a black brigade or treating his presidential oath of office "as a practical joke, and suspend[ing] the Constitution."[89] His plan for reconstruction was a "grim joke" that ignored "the vested rights of State and Constitutional Law."[90] The *New York Herald* warned Lincoln's presidential rivals to beware "his uncontrollable love of fun," which would fashion "the plot of choking them all before the next election."[91]

The Election of 1864

The voices of complaint about the national joker in the White House, which grew steadily louder during the first three years of Lincoln's presidency, became a vehement chorus of condemnation during 1864, as he sought renomination and then reelection. The themes did not alter, but antiadministration presses and opposition political platforms asserted them with more aggression and imaginative color than ever.

The election contest was explicitly joined in the opening weeks of the year. Bryant's positive appreciation of Lincoln's humor in the pages of the *Evening Post* drew from James Gordon Bennett's *New York Herald* the headline "The Presidential Campaign. The First Electioneering Document." The claim was both teasing and disingenuous: Bryant, though lukewarm about the president's renomination, had been responding to an assault on Lincoln "the smutty joker" already launched in the pages of the *Herald*. With moves afoot among Republicans to deliver the party's nomination to John C. Frémont,

Bennett ran a long article, "General Fremont Takes the Presidential Field—Not a Smutty Joker." Setting out the general's claims as a military leader and emancipator, the *Herald* followed each positive statement with the bald refrain, repeated thirty times over, "Fremont is not a smutty joker." The maverick Bennett hoped that the general or some other candidate would emerge as the unanimous choice of the party, "and thus save all trouble, astonish all Europe, overawe the rebellion and prevent us from having a smutty joker for our next President." Every age had its great joker, the *Herald* subsequently reflected. In Lincoln—"a joke incarnated"—America had produced its own bawdy genius to rival Boccacio and Joe Miller: his election, presidency, entry into society, emancipation proclamation, and actions as commander in chief were all sorry jokes. Measured by his own criteria for office—"one who can tell a real old side splitter and skull cracker"—his most formidable rival for the nomination would be Miles O'Reilly.[92]

An increase in such assaults during the run-up to the Union party's nominating convention in Baltimore was encouraged by the distaste of fellow Republicans for a vacillating president who took jocular refuge in "some smutty story."[93] The country had been *"willing to laugh at Mr. Lincoln's jokes for a season,"* declared the *Spirit of the Times*, but now it could no longer tolerate "some jocose clodpole" at the helm.[94] In the *Funniest of Phun* and *Harper's Weekly* (Figure 5), the radical cartoonist Frank Bellew cast Lincoln as the National Joker, a circus jester who was reminded of "a little joke" and "another little story." In one image, he stands grinning under three wartime scenes—the hospital, the battlefield, and Liberty consumed by flames—each pointing out the grotesque contrast between unpresidential levity and martial horror. From the other end of the political spectrum, an Indiana voice regretted that the historic fool of the royal courts of Europe, long since obsolete, had been revived in Washington: some might think that "if we are to have a merryandrew for President, Old Abe ought to give way" to a circus clown like "Dan Rice, Sol. Lipman, Jim Ross, or Nat. Austin."[95]

Characteristically, Lincoln acknowledged his renomination in June with a joke. He told the National Union delegates who called on him that their renewed confidence did not mean "that I am the best man in the country," but he was reminded "of a story of an old Dutch farmer who remarked to a companion once that 'it was not best to swap horses when crossing streams.'"[96] This was not a new story, nor was it the first time Lincoln had used it, but it was not stale enough to deny him the laughter he intended. It gave more ammunition to his critics, however: the "boisterous guffaws" promoted by this example of "untimely mirth" were evidence of "the empty mind" of "the heartless buffoon and his parasite." Even loyalists worried that Lincoln thought his nomination gave him "full . . . license to repeat all his old jokes"; if he had to have a story for every occasion he should get an entirely new set, but "it would add materially to the dignity of his position if he would leave off his jokes altogether till he retires from the Presidency."[97] Others scoffed at the inconsistencies in the president's metaphor. After all, he had seen "no objection to swapping generals, to exchange McClellan for Pope, McClellan for Burnside, Burnside for Hooker, Hooker for Meade," or in changing the members of his administration, or in switching candidates for vice-president.[98] A Boston clergyman cast the joke against Lincoln by noting that although Moses got the children of Israel out of Egypt, "the Lord selected somebody else to bring them to their journey's end."[99]

Setting the tone for Peace Democrats' assaults on Lincoln was the striking front cover of Andrew Adderup's *Lincolniana, or Humors of Uncle Abe: Second Joe Miller.* The author's pseudonym was a weak joke: "adderup" appears above an image of a copperhead snake. Published by the staunch Copperhead J. F. Feeks, the book turns Lincoln's popular reputation into a weapon against the administration. Axe in hand, the lover of the English jester drives a wedge—labeled 'Joke'—into a log that is splitting into north and south: the rail-splitter and side-splitter here becomes the Union-splitter (Figure 6). Attacks on the "ribald jester" and "coarse filthy joker" continued, intensifying after the Democrats selected McClellan as their presidential nominee at Chicago in late August. The "undignified, jesting, negro fanatic," who could "crack jokes like a Nero while Rome is burning," had had greatness thrust upon him, yet "the smutty joker always peeps out from underneath," revealing "the incapable dwarf who tries to play the part of a giant."[100] The banners decorating the McClellan ratification meetings in September lauded the general as "the White Man's President," while castigating Lincoln as a tyrannical emancipator and a worn-out joker, more fit for Barnum's museum than the presidency. "This reminds me of a joke," proclaimed a banner in Cincinnati, with a caricature of the president prompting laughter from an old horse. Others declared "Old Abe can't see this joke" and "No Vulgar Joker for President."[101]

Democrats insinuated a critique of Lincoln the Joker into each of their key campaigning themes of 1864: the administration's perverted racial radicalism, its tyrannical assault on civil liberties, and its generally demoralizing influence. None was more challenging than the charge of Lincoln's shocking levity in the face of the summer's numbing military slaughter. Even before the unprecedented carnage of the Wilderness, Spotsylvania, and Cold Harbor, he invited the protest "Every joke of Mr. Lincoln has cost 100,000 lives and $150,000,000. The nation has been joked to death."[102] German voices lamented that "while streams of blood are being spilled unnecessarily, . . . Lincoln continues telling us his stories, and asks actor Hackett to produce Falstaff before him!"[103] The *Chicago Times*, never slow to embroider or even manufacture a story, attributed Grant's bloody campaign in Virginia to a White House conclave: "the bottle went freely around. Mr Lincoln was in 'his best vein,' and anecdote and 'smutty joke' followed each other in quick succession."[104] A Philadelphia newspaper lamented that while Washington's streets "were vocal with the groans of the wounded," the "Springfield joker entertained a deputation of clergymen with a coarse story about Grant's 'intending to fight it out on that line, if he had to fight all summer.'" Yet these "reverend hypocrites laughed and nudged each other," sanctifying the words uttered by the "chosen of God."[105] Another despaired, "Why should the jester mourn with the afflicted, when his parasites are laughing at his ribald jokes?"[106]

At the Democratic national convention William Allen, ex-governor of Ohio, set out the stark electoral choice. The people did not want "a cold-blooded joker" who, "when he can spare a minute from Joe Miller's jest book, looks out upon the acres of hospitals and inquires 'What houses are those!'" McClellan, however, would not answer soldiers "with a ribald joke." Union troops would be cared for, their pensions paid, and their families looked after.[107] The theme of Lincoln "the widow-maker who lays the nation across his knee and tickles her catastrophe with obscene jokes and little stories" remained a campaign staple.[108]

Nothing gave that assault more persisting power than one particular accusation: that when visiting the blood-drenched Antietam battlefield in October 1862 Lincoln had behaved with blasphemous contempt for its sanctity. The charge had been leveled during the previous year, but only in the summer and fall of 1864 did Democratic propagandists use their creative imaginations to exploit it to the full. At the center of the several versions stood the claim that with astonishing but characteristic insensitivity, the ribald president had asked to hear a vulgar comic song while touring the field of battle. According to the *World,* among the staunchest of New York's Democratic presses, the incident took place just a few days after the fight, with bodies "yet warm in their freshly-made graves."[109] Accompanied by Ward Hill Lamon, General McClellan, and another officer, Lincoln drove over the field in an ambulance as "heavy details of men" were burying the dead. As they neared the old stone bridge, "where the bodies were piled highest," Lincoln, "suddenly slapping Marshal Lamon upon the knee, exclaimed: 'Come, Lamon! give us that song about 'Picayune Butler.' McClellan has never heard it." With a shudder, the General protested, "Not now, if you please Marshal. . . . I would prefer to hear it some other place and time."[110]

The story assumed various forms. One had Lincoln present at the battle itself. Readers learned that with his ears "filled with the shrieks of the wounded and the dying," he asked "his private secretary to play 'Jim Crow' upon the fiddle."[111] Another version described a sly president preparing to betray his general-in-chief: by cracking "festive jokes in the ears of the dying," he hid "his treacherous purpose of moving the commander who had saved his army, and returned to Washington only to carry out his fatal purpose."[112] Few accounts failed to emphasize Lincoln's taste for "a negro song": "Picayune

Butler's Coming to Town," a popular African American banjo song often performed by blackface minstrels, confirmed his vulgarity and perverted racial appetites. The *Cincinnati Daily Enquirer* made Lincoln a figure in a Faustian drama, his savage humor and pursuit of "a nigger war for abolition" echoed by a chilling operatic chorus: "HA! HA! HA! *Nobody Hurt!* Hark! What's this? The ambulances are passing. Hear those groans. . . . Give us Picayune Butler, Marshal Lamon. Hear the chorus: HA! HA! HA! *Nobody Hurt.*" But "one hundred and fifty thousand widows and five hundred thousand little orphan children demand that the tyrant take his hand off the throat of our nation."[113]

Democrats hammered the message in music and graphic satire. As described in the crude rhymes of the *Democratic National Campaign Songster*, one of the many low publications emerging from J. F. Feeks's New York Copperhead press, "Honest Old Abe was a queer old coon, / Joked with a nigger and play'd the buffoon." Others declared,

> A ruined land that once was grand,
> Is not a joking matter—
> Though Abe we know, the more our woe,
> The more his jokes he'll chatter!

This theme easily accommodated the Antietam episode. Democrats chanted, "Old Uncle Abe is a used up babe, With all his jokes and toddy," and declared that

> Our 'Little Mac' is just the man
> To restore the nation's glories;
> He never will on battle-field
> Indulge in smutty stories."[114]

A song whose first verse paid tribute to Mac's victory at Antietam launched the second with a stinging rebuke:

> Abe may crack his jolly jokes,
>   O'er bloody fields of stricken battle
> While yet the ebbing life-tide smokes
>   From men that die like butchered cattle;

He, ere yet the guns grow cold,
 To pimps and pets may crack his stories;
Your name is of the grander mould,
 And linked with all our brightest glories![115]

The 1864 campaign gave political cartoonists unbridled opportunity to exploit the familiar theme of Lincoln's compulsive and regrettable jesting. In Joseph E. Baker's lithograph "Columbia Demands Her Children," an angry Columbia points at a discomfited president and shouts, "Mr LINCOLN, give me back my 500,000 sons!!!" which elicits a feeble, diversionary response: "Well, the fact is—by the way that reminds me of a STORY!!!" A Currier and Ives cartoon, "Running the 'Machine,'" has Lincoln laughing uproariously at his own jokes, while the new secretary of the treasury, William Pitt Fessenden, churns out greenbacks (Figure 7). A later print from the same stable, "Abraham's Dream: 'Coming Events Cast Their Shadows Before,'" depicts Lincoln facing the nightmare of his ejection from the White House with the words "This don't remind me of any joke!!" After McClellan's nomination, a J. H. Howard cartoon characterized the Democratic candidate as Hamlet, contemplating Lincoln's laughing head on the palm of his hand and saying to Governor Seymour, "I knew him Horatio; a fellow of infinite jests. *** Where be your gibes now?" Few depictions of the gleeful president were more arresting, however, than the sinister portrayal "Columbia's Nightmare" by Matt Morgan in the British magazine *Fun.* Inspired by Henry Fuseli's *The Nightmare,* the cartoon shows Lincoln as a smirking, Semitic demon seated on a terrified recumbent maiden. This was humor of the darkest kind (Figure 8).

Above all, however, it was the Antietam episode that offered the best target of graphic attack. Rally banners in Cincinnati depicted Lincoln—not Marshal Lamon—singing "Picayune Butler," with hundreds of dead and wounded soldiers lying around him and a Union regiment behind.[116] Especially potent was a poorly executed but still arresting cartoon headed "The Commander-in-Chief Conciliates the Soldier's Vote on the Battlefield." Published in New York just a month before the election, it placed Lincoln at the center, clad in a long cloak and holding a tartan cap—a reminder of "the coward's disguise" he was said to have worn when cutting short his journey to Washington as president-elect. Several of the dead bodies are being carried from the field while an officer—evidently McClellan—tends to a wounded soldier. A distraught figure, his back to the viewer, signals his distress by holding a hand to his eyes; he remonstrates as the president demands, "Now, Marshall, sing us 'Picayune Butler,' or something else that's funny" (Figure 9).

Lincoln loyalists took alarm at the tightening grip of the bogus story on the public imagination and asked the White House to expose the Copperheads' "abominable lie."[117] Lamon prepared a reply for the press that Lincoln considered too bellicose. "I would give the statement as you have it without the cussedness," the president told him. "Let me try my hand at it." In a careful draft, designed to appear over Lamon's signature, he rebutted the false account by setting out "the whole story of the singing." While traveling on an ambulance from Antietam to General Fitz John Porter's corps, Lincoln wrote, "the President asked me to sing the little sad song ['Twenty Years Ago'] . . . which he had often heard me sing." Then "some one of the party, (I do not think it was the President) asked me to sing something else; and I sang two or three little comic things of which Picayune Butler was one." However, "the place was not on the battle field, the time was sixteen days after the battle, no dead body was seen during the whole time the president was absent from Washington, nor even a grave that had not been rained on since it was made." Lincoln explained, with equal emphasis, "Neither Gen. McClellan [n]or any one else made any objection to the singing."[118]

On reflection, however, Lincoln decided against releasing his account, telling Lamon, "You know, Hill, that this is the truth and the whole truth about that affair, but I dislike to appear as an apologist for an act of my own which I know was right."[119] The marshal himself made use of Lincoln's statement, but only in private correspondence. Reassuring a Philadelphian that the story was quite untrue, he added that it was "a source of congratulation to me that so much has been attempted to be made out of such slender material"—a sign of the Democrats' electoral desperation.[120] Lincoln evidently shared his opinion. Toward the end of September the head of the Washington office of the *New York Tribune* asked John G. Nicolay whether Lincoln deemed the attacks worthy of a response and, if so, to suggest the most profitable form of reply.[121] The *Tribune*'s offer was not taken up.

The Democrats' assault on Lincoln's obscenity, vulgarity, and levity during the dark days of summer did nothing to help improve the president's reelection prospects. By late August the Republican campaign's high command had lost hope of his victory in November. Even so, his supporters denied that he was a "mere joker." How could a man who refused to uncouple the policies of emancipation and reunion be anything other than "a man of deep convictions, of abiding faith in justice, truth and Providence"? After visiting the White House that month, Joseph T. Mills recorded an encouraging meeting: "The President appeared to be not the pleasant joker I had expected to see, but a man of deep convictions & an unutterable yearning for the success of the Union cause. . . . I could not but feel . . . that I stood in the presence of the great guiding intellect of the age." Instead of vulgarity, here was "transparent honesty, . . . republican simplicity, . . . gushing sympathy for those who offered their lives for their country, [and] utter forgetfulness of self."[122]

The political weather changed dramatically during early September. The fall of Atlanta, the broader evidence of Union military progress, and the Democrats' adoption of a peace platform buoyed the hopes of Union loyalists. As confidence in Lincoln's reelection grew, high-profile War Democrats joined Republicans in rebutting Copperhead calumnies. David S. Coddington explained that "the Chicago convention has left a Democrat no choice between Jefferson Davis, with all his crimes, and Abraham Lincoln, with all his faults. . . . Call Abraham Lincoln a joker! Why the Chicago party are trying to make this war the ghastliest joke of the continent or century."[123] Elect that ticket, he said, "and you elect a laugh at your own arrogance, imbecility and cowardice; you elect an acknowledgment that eight millions of people, armed with an impracticable sophistry are too much for twenty millions backed by the eternal truths of republican faith and national sovereignty."[124] Speaking in Indiana, a New York judge defended Lincoln "as an instrument of

Almighty God to accomplish the great work . . . of preserving for all time to come, our wonderful Government." Lauding the president's "undying good humor" as an "almost miraculous endowment," he commended his "proverbial and endless" jokes and parables: "good, unctuous, witty, humorous, human, . . . they hurt nobody and please every body. If he is ever satirical, what pains he takes to extract the sting! Surely no man ever lived who, more uniformly, was guarded least he should wound the feelings of his fellow man."[125]

In keeping with the changed mood, poster cartoons sympathetic to the National Union Party turned the joke against the Democratic nominee. "McClellan Tries to Ride Two Horses" played on the equine metaphor that Lincoln had put into play with his joke about swapping steeds in midstream. "Little Mac" appears as a star-spangled circus rider struggling to keep a foot on each horse. The president looks on, clad in clown's motley, but unsmiling and serious. McClellan has one hand pulling on the reins of a war charger straining for action and is tugged in the other direction by a horse labeled "peace." He curses them, saying, "I can't manage the Act no how." Lincoln's sharp words—"You tried to ride them two hosses on the Peninsula for two years Mac but it wouldn't work"—drew attention to the historic roots of the deep division at Chicago between McClellan and the peace wing of his party[126] (Figure 10). More demeaning still in its portrayal of McClellan was a *Harper's Weekly* cartoon of the Little Napoleon as a diminutive plaything standing on the palm of Lincoln's cupped hand. Seated at his desk in the chief executive's chair, the president addresses the tiny general with words that turned the laugh against his opponent: "This reminds me of a little joke."[127]

There is no way of determining precisely how Lincoln's reputation as a joker and storyteller shaped the political balance sheet in 1864. That the administration's supporters included many who found the president's levity distasteful indicates that, for them at least, the matter was not decisive. His opponents, on the other hand, clearly believed it offered great electoral opportunity. Their focus on the cruel and smutty joker during the final weeks of the campaign should not be seen simply as a measure of increasing desperation as the electoral tide flowed against them, since their relish for the issue had been evident well before their hopes went into decline. Moreover, Lincoln, too, well understood how his reputation for levity could expose him to personal misrepresentation and electoral damage: it was only after careful weighing of the consequences that he opted not to respond publicly to the bogus Antietam story. In time, after his death, his reputation as the peerless presidential story spinner, joke teller, and ready wit would come to take on a character wholly positive and benign. That, however, was not the reality during the dark and deadly days of war.

Figure 1. Cover of *Old Abe's Joker, or Wit at the White House.* New York: R. M. De Witt, 1863.

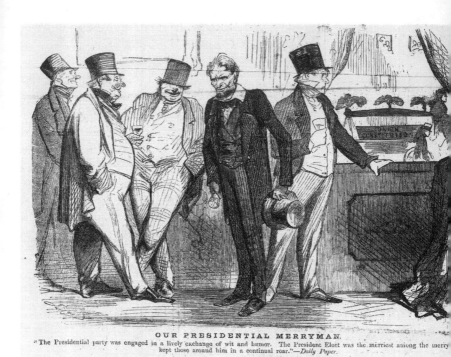

OUR PRESIDENTIAL MERRYMAN.

"The Presidential party was engaged in a lively exchange of wit and humor. The President Elect was the merriest among the merry kept those around him in a continual roar."—*Daily Paper*.

Figure 2. "Our Presidential Merryman." *Harper's Weekly*, March 2, 1861. Library of Congress.

Figure 3. "Comedy of Death." Adalbert Volck, July 1861.

Figure 4. "'Where Are My 15,000 Sons?' Columbia Confronts Her Children." *Harper's Weekly*, January 3, 1863.

Figure 5. Frank Bellew, "The National Joker. Salary $25,000 per annum." *Harper's Weekly*, April 2, 1864.

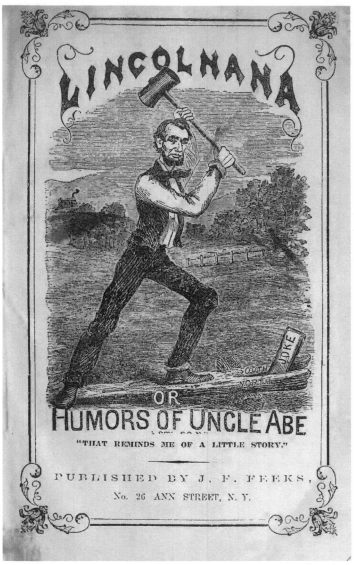

Figure 6. Cover of Andrew Adderup, *Lincoln[i]ana, or Humors of Uncle Abe: Second Joe Miller*. New York: J. F. Feeks, 1864.

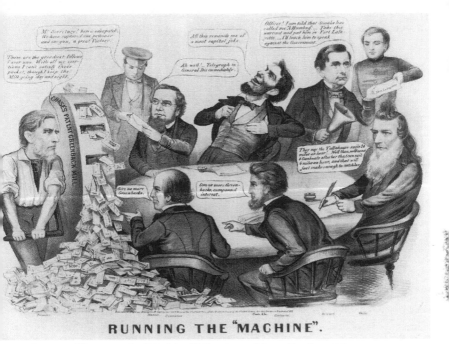

Figure 7. "Running the 'Machine.'" Currier and Ives, October, 1864.
Library of Congress.

Figure 8. "Columbia's Nightmare." Matt Morgan, *Fun*, September 10, 1864.

Figure 9. "The Commander-in-Chief Conciliates the Soldier's Votes." Unknown artist, New York, October 1864. Library of Congress.

Figure 10. "McClellan Tries to Ride Two Horses." National Union Party Cartoon, 1864. Library of Congress.

EPILOGUE

Lincoln's last conscious moments were filled with laughter. As everyone familiar with his history knows, he spent his last evening at Ford's Theatre, watching Tom Taylor's popular farce *Our American Cousin*. Just days after Robert E. Lee's surrender, this was fitting entertainment for a president who had told his wife that with the return of peace they "must *both,* be more cheerful in the future." His assassin, John Wilkes Booth, waited until the delivery of a line in the play's final act that he knew would prompt enough laughter to muffle his shot. The last words the president heard were "Well, I guess I know enough to turn you inside out, old gal—you sockdologizing old mantrap." Taylor's colorful coinage was an extension of "sockdolager"—a knockout blow—itself a term of very recent invention. Lincoln, with his appetite for fresh and idiomatic language, would have savored the joke. The circumstances of the death of a laughter-loving president could not have been more wretchedly poignant.

The administration's enemies on the home front rejoiced that the murder had rid the country of a jesting tyrant. Clearly, a Wisconsin newspaper concluded, God had "wanted Lincoln removed," and "made Booth His agent." If Lincoln were now in Heaven, as his friends maintained, then let God be thanked for calling him there— "into the presence and company of Democrats"—and releasing him from the capital's plague of "thieves, Abolitionists, army contractors, office-seekers and gaping listeners to his smutty jokes." Consequently, "the country is better off now than when Lincoln was alive. We believe more in statesmanship than in nigger songs, or in humorous yarns in time of war."[1]

The prevailing public mood, however, was grief at the loss of a great and wise leader whose sense of humor had been an essential element of his character. Sorrowing speakers recognized that humor had been "as natural to him as breathing," "as natural as his pulse," and had "kept his temper sweet." A Boston minister offered a graphic image: "This quaint, ever-ready humor was the soft cushion upon which the great burdens of his public cares impinged, covering and shielding his nerves from laceration." It delivered a wider benefit, too. The Congregationalist minister Joseph P. Thompson lauded Lincoln's stories as "philosophy in parables," and his jests as morals. Another described how they "conciliated those who differed from him. He could convince with a smile, refute with a jest, turn the flank of heavy reasoning with this agile lightness of wit and conquer kind feeling." As the comic writer Robert H. Newell put it in his poetic lament, *The Martyr President*, "No more shall the eye ever bright with a smile, / Bring light to the honest, confusion to guile."[2] For the Methodist Gilbert Haven, Lincoln's "merry twinkle," even in saddest sorrow, put him alongside other great men: "Napoleon, Socrates, Cicero, Caesar, Wesley, Franklin, Webster."[3]

For the next forty years or so after his death those who had been close to Lincoln honored his reputation for humor by adding examples to the treasury of his stories. They included Henry J. Raymond, editor of the *New York Times;* the painter Francis N. Carpenter; William H. Herndon and his scores of informants; Joshua F. Speed, Lincoln's intimate; Ward Hill Lamon, his friend and bodyguard; Noah Brooks, newspaperman and regular White House visitor; Isaac N. Arnold, congressional ally; and Henry C. Whitney, fellow lawyer and circuit rider. There were many others besides, including contributors to the compilations of Osborne H. I. Oldroyd, a devoted collector, and Allen Thorndike Rice, the editor of the *North American Review*.[4] By no means were all the offerings reliably authentic, but their claim on posterity is less suspect than many later additions to the compendium of Lincoln's humor, above all the many commercial compilations of his wit and wisdom with which publishers have helped fuel the public appetite for his jokes and stories.

Lincoln's reputation as humorist enjoyed a modest boost during the general enhancement of his reputation early in the twentieth century, when—through the encouragement of Theodore Roosevelt and Woodrow Wilson—he came to be seen as the first Progressive, the defender of the rights of ordinary people against corporate power and privilege. Lincoln's storytelling and love of humor helped crystallize his popular identity as an accessible and unpretentious representative of the underdog, the common man with simple tastes.[5] Yet the broader reevaluation of his significance at the same time shaped a contrasting and more potent image: the peerless statesman, high-minded political philosopher, and earnest poet. As expressed in the Lincoln Memorial in Washington, D.C., and above all in Daniel French's monumental sculpture, the sixteenth president loses every trace of the levity and jocularity that had defined him during his lifetime.

Since Lincoln's death, the waters have gradually closed over the complex reality of his sense of humor—its range, multiple purposes, and capacity to offend as well as entertain and instruct. This process was assisted by friends and associates who wanted to protect his reputation by excising the dubious stories and smutty jokes. Abner Y. Ellis happily told Herndon that he had no difficulty in recalling these, "but Modesty and my Veneration for his Memory forbids me to relate [them]."[6] Acquaintances who had less fond recollections made known their distaste, but did so within a wrapping of praise for Lincoln's other qualities. Henry Villard had found it impossible, he wrote, to "take a real personal liking to the man," and had felt "disgust and humiliation that such a person"—with an "inborn weakness" for coarse jokes, "low talk," and "repulsive fiction"—should be entrusted with the destiny of a great nation in its direst crisis. Yet Villard deodorized his memoir, denying that the president's conversation was predominantly trivial and vulgar: "his was really a very sober and serious nature, and even inclined to gloominess."[7]

Even more significant, with the passage of time Lincoln's stories and jokes floated free from the moorings of their original setting.

Increasingly detached from the context that had given them their particular political and cultural bite, they lost much of the didactic, ironic, and satiric meaning that he had intended and enjoyed. Their force and sharpness had served him well socially and professionally. They had been valuable in advancing his public career as politician and lawyer, and in navigating his course during a storm-tossed presidency; at the same time, not only were these weapons dangerously double-edged, but a reputation for unrestrained, uncontrollable humor also gave welcome ammunition to his political foes. When dehistoricized, romanticized, and supplemented by apocrypha, Lincoln's humor loses much of its original and authentic richness. Helping to recapture that complexity has been the animating purpose of this book.

ACKNOWLEDGMENTS

In keeping with the distinctive purpose of the Concise Lincoln Library, these acknowledgments will be "short and sweet, like the old woman's dance" (as the young Lincoln famously described his politics). My thanks are no less sincere for that. Sylvia Rodrigue kindly invited me to write this book and has been remarkably patient in waiting for it. Corpus Christi College granted me a term's sabbatical release from the presidency to take up a productive short-term research fellowship at the Huntington Library, San Marino, California. Two very fine postgraduate research assistants, Nichola Clayton and Steve Tuffnell, gave me outstanding help. I have benefited not only from Michael Burlingame's voluminous scholarship but also his solicitude and generous suggestions. Paul M. Zall's encyclopedic collections of Lincoln's jokes and Wayne Lee Garner's undeservedly neglected doctoral dissertation have been especially valuable. Other scholars who have helped shape my thinking include Gerald J. Prokopowicz, the late Elizabeth Brown Pryor, Brian Steele, Douglas L. Wilson, and my Oxford colleagues Gareth Davies, Donald Ratcliffe, Jay Sexton, and Stephen Tuck. Robert Cook and Stephen E. Maizlish commented on the whole manuscript with gracious discernment; I have benefited, too, from the suggestions of Southern Illinois University Press's anonymous readers and the series editors. I have also been blessed by the superlative copyediting of Wayne Larsen, the professionalism of my favorite indexer, Andrea Greengrass, and the valuable secretarial help of Sara Watson. I am grateful for opportunities to try out my ideas on several audiences, including the American Religious History Workshop at Princeton University, as Visiting Stewart Fellow; the European Association for American Studies biennial conference at The Hague; and the American History Research Seminars in Cambridge University and the Rothermere American Institute, Oxford. Portions of chapter 3 are adapted from *Lincoln's Just Laughter: Humour and Ethics in the Civil War Union*, the Second Eccles Centre for American Studies Plenary Lecture (London: British Library, 2014). The book is dedicated fondly to my Oxford undergraduate tutor and graduate supervisor, John Walsh, who introduced me to the scholarly allure of Abraham Lincoln and his era, guided my early uncertain steps in religious history, and has been a lifelong, inspiring example. My greatest debt is to my wife, Linda Kirk, a loving but clear-eyed critic of all that I write.

NOTES

ALLL   Paul M. Zall, ed. *Abe Lincoln's Legacy of Laughter: Humorous Stories by and about Abraham Lincoln.* Knoxville: University of Tennessee Press, 2007.

ALP   Abraham Lincoln Papers, Library of Congress.

Burlingame   Michael Burlingame. *Abraham Lincoln: A Life,* 2 vols. Baltimore: Johns Hopkins University Press, 2008.

Burlingame [online]   Michael Burlingame. *Abraham Lincoln: A Life*, the Unedited Manuscript. Lincoln Studies Center, Knox College, Galesburg, Illinois. https://www.knox.edu/about-knox/lincoln-studies-center/burlingame-abraham-lincoln-a-life.

CW   *The Collected Works of Abraham Lincoln.* Edited by Roy P. Basler. 9 vols. New Brunswick, NJ: Rutgers University Press, 1953–55.

Garner   Wayne Lee Garner. "Abraham Lincoln and the Uses of Humor." PhD dissertation. Iowa State University, 1963.

Herndon's Lincoln   William H. Herndon and Jesse Weik. *Herndon's Lincoln.* Edited by Douglas L. Wilson and Rodney O. Davis. Urbana: University of Illinois Press, 2006.

HI   Douglas L. Wilson, Rodney O. Davis, and Terry Wilson, eds. *Herndon's Informants: Letters, Interviews, and Statements about Abraham Lincoln.* Urbana: University of Illinois Press, 1998.

LCHL   Lincoln Collection, Huntington Library, San Marino, Calif.

Rice   Allen Thorndike Rice, ed. *Reminiscences of Abraham Lincoln by Distinguished Men of His Time.* New York, 1886.

RWAL   Don E. Fehrenbacher and Virginia Fehrenbacher, comps. and eds. *Recollected Words of Abraham Lincoln.* Stanford, Calif.: Stanford University Press, 1996.

Introduction

1. *Appletons' Journal of Literature, Science, and Art* 3, no. 61 (May 1870), 615.
2. Garner, 616.
3. Sloane, *Humor in the White House*, 93–94, 165–68, 183.

4. Norman A. Graebner, "Commentary on 'Abe Lincoln Laughing,'" in Boritt, *Historian's Lincoln*, 19; Randall, *Lincoln the President*, 67; Wagenknecht, *Abraham Lincoln,* 571.

5. *Herndon's Lincoln*, 351.

6. *HI*, 348.

7. Grinnell, *Men and Events*, 171.

8. See, among many examples, Guelzo, *Abraham Lincoln: Redeemer President*; Wilson, *Honor's Voice*, 126.

9. Randall, *Lincoln the President: Midstream*, 67.

10. Neely, *Boundaries of American Political Culture*; Stott, *Jolly Fellows*.

11. For example, Carpenter, *Six Months*; McClure, *"Abe" Lincoln's Yarns and Stories*.

12. *ALLL;* Zall, *Abe Lincoln Laughing*.

13. *New York Herald*, February 19, 1864.

14. Jones, introduction to *Struggles of Petroleum V. Nasby*, xvi–xvii.

15. Evans, "Humour of History," 44–58.

16. Stewart, *Wendell Phillips*, 240; *New York Herald*, February 19, July 7, 1864; Neely, "Commentary on 'Abe Lincoln Laughing,'" in Boritt, *Historian's Lincoln*, 28.

17. Faust, *This Republic of Suffering* (drawing on Frederick Law Olmsted).

18. Burlingame and Ettlinger, *Inside Lincoln's White House*, 73.

19. *HI*, 157–58 (Joshua F. Speed).

1. The Face and Phases of Lincoln's Humor

1. Harris, "Recollections," scrapbook 45, p. 10, LCHL.

2. Whitney, "Abraham Lincoln," 464–66.

3. Conant, "Portrait Painter's Reminiscences," 512.

4. McBride, *Personal Recollections*, 46–47.

5. *HI*, 698 (Horace White).

6. Carpenter, *Six Months*, 150.

7. Strong, *Diary*, 3:188.

8. Harris, "Recollections," scrapbook 45, p. 10, LCHL. Cf. Chrisman, *Memoirs of Lincoln*, 61–62.

9. Villard, *Memoirs*, 1:143.

10. Brooks, "Personal Reminiscences," 564.

11. Copybook Verses [1824–1826], *CW*, 1:1.

12. *HI*, 109; Remsburg, *Abraham Lincoln*, 197.

13. *HI*, 102–9 (A. H. Chapman; Dennis Hanks; Sarah Bush Lincoln).

14. *Herndon's Lincoln*, 44–49; *HI*, 151–52 (Elizabeth Crawford); Bray, "Power to Hurt"; Kaplan, *Biography of a Writer*, 38–40; Lincoln, "Speech in U.S. House of Representatives on the Presidential Question," July 27, 1848, *CW*, 1:509.

15. *HI,* 373, 429, 457, 607 (John Hanks); Tarbell, *Lincoln,* 1:52–53.
16. *HI,* 370, 539.
17. Onstot, *Pioneers,* 375–76.
18. Burlingame, *Oral History,* 8–9; *HI,* 6–7.
19. *HI,* 363.
20. Ibid., 330 (George M. Harrison).
21. Ibid., 18.
22. Ibid., 13 (Hardin Bale).
23. Ibid., 540 (Jason Duncan).
24. Burlingame [online], 1:277.
25. *HI,* 540 (Jason Duncan).
26. Nicolay, "Lincoln's Literary Experiments," 824–25.
27. *Herndon's Lincoln,* 115–16; *HI,* 477–78, 589 (Joshua F. Speed).
28. Holland, *Life of Abraham Lincoln,* 66–67.
29. Stevens, *Reporter's Lincoln,* 114.
30. Arnold, *Life of Abraham Lincoln,* 82–83.
31. Bridges, "Three Letters," 87.
32. Stevens, *Reporter's Lincoln,* 98.
33. *Herndon's Lincoln,* 130; *HI,* 239 (Samuel C. Parks); Burlingame, 1:156.
34. Whitney, "Abraham Lincoln," 477; Wilson, *Honor's Voice,* 175–78, 265–76, 298–304.
35. Burlingame, 1:135.
36. Burlingame [online], 1:499.
37. Lincoln, "The 'Rebecca' Letter," August 27, 1842, *CW,* 1:295–96.
38. James Shields to Lincoln, September 17, 1842, *CW,* 1:299–300.
39. Burlingame [online], 1:570.
40. Lincoln, "Memorandum of Duel Instructions to Elias H. Merryman," September 19, 1842, *CW,* 1:300–301.
41. Lincoln to Martin S. Morris, March 26, 1843, *CW,* 1:320.
42. Wilson, *Honor's Voice,* 303–4.
43. Burlingame, 1:158.
44. Lincoln, "Remarks in Illinois Legislature concerning a Bill for Completion of the Illinois and Michigan Canal," February 26, 1841, *CW,* 1:243–44.
45. Browne, *Every-Day Life of Abraham Lincoln,* 171.
46. Rice, 219–21.
47. Lincoln, "Speech in U.S. House of Representatives on the Presidential Question," July 27, 1848, *CW,* 1:507–12.
48. Ibid., 1:512–14.
49. *HI,* 699; Lincoln, "Speech at Worcester, Massachusetts," September 12, 1848, *CW,* 2:3.
50. Lincoln, "Speech at Boston, Massachusetts," September 15, 1848, *CW,* 2:5.

51. Burlingame [online], 1:757.

52. Busey, *Personal Reminiscences*, 25–28.

53. Rice, 217–18, 222.

54. Whitney, "Abraham Lincoln," 473.

55. Burlingame [online], 1:921.

56. Stevens, *Reporter's Lincoln*, 34.

57. Burlingame [online], 1:961.

58. *Herndon's Lincoln*, 395.

59. *HI*, 181 (Joseph Gillespie).

60. Schurz, *Reminiscences*, 2:215.

61. Johannsen, *Douglas*, 641.

62. Edward Francis Test, "Lincoln and Douglas," typescript, p. 9, HM 39723, Huntington Library.

63. *ALLL*, xiii.

64. Lincoln, "Speech at Springfield, Illinois," July 17, 1858, *CW*, 2:506.

65. Garner, 283.

66. Lincoln, "Sixth Debate with Stephen A. Douglas, at Quincy, Illinois," October 13, 1858, *CW*, 3:279.

67. Lincoln, "Fourth Debate with Stephen A. Douglas at Charleston, Illinois," September 18, 1858, *CW*, 3:184.

68. Lincoln, "First Debate with Stephen A. Douglas at Ottawa, Illinois," August 21, 1858, *CW*, 3:16.

69. Lincoln, "Fourth Debate with Stephen A. Douglas at Charleston, Illinois," September 18, 1858, *CW*, 3:178.

70. Lincoln, "First Debate with Stephen A. Douglas at Ottawa, Illinois," August 21, 1858, *CW*, 3:17, 20.

71. *CW*, 3:356–57; Winger, *Lincoln, Religion, and Romantic Cultural Politics*, 23.

72. Conway, *Autobiography*, 1:317.

73. Burlingame [online], 1:1599–600.

74. Burlingame [online], 1:1615–16.

75. Garner, 321–22.

76. Lincoln, "Speech at New Haven, Connecticut," March 6, 1860, *CW*, 4:16, 21.

77. *CW*, 4:12–13.

78. Stevens, *Reporter's Lincoln*, 95–96.

79. Villard, *Memoirs*, 1:143; Burlingame [online], 1:1882–83; Holzer, *Lincoln and the Power of the Press*, 271–72.

80. Lincoln, "Remarks at Thorntown and Lebanon, Indiana," February 11, 1861, *CW*, 4:192–93.

81. *RWAL*, 53.

82. *ALLL*, xii.

83. Lincoln, "Remarks to Citizens of Gettysburg, Pennsylvania," November 18, 1863, *CW*, 7:16–17.
84. *HI*, 361.
85. Stoddard, *Inside the White House*, 190.
86. Burlingame [online], 2:3480.
87. Noah Brooks, "Personal Recollections," 226.
88. Burlingame [online], 2:3743.
89. Carpenter, *Six Months*, 293.
90. McCulloch, *Men and Measures*, 222.

2. Sources, Species, Subjects

1. Rice, 428; Brooks, "Personal Recollections," 228; Villard, *Memoirs*, 1:143.
2. *HI*, 37, 96, 137, 598.
3. Burlingame [online], 1:14.
4. Whitney, *Life on the Circuit*, 179.
5. Rice, 428.
6. Burlingame, 2:74.
7. Burlingame [online], 2:3263–64.
8. *HI*, 251, 420, 470 (James H. Matheny, John McNemar).
9. Speed, *Reminiscences*, 31–32. The love-struck lion had allowed the removal of his claws and teeth as the price of marriage to the maiden; he was then clubbed to death by her father.
10. Tarbell, "Humor in the White House," 7–8, Tarbell Collection, Allegheny College; Baldwin, *Flush Times of Alabama and Mississippi*, 155; Derby, *Phoenixiana, or Sketches and Burlesques*.
11. Bray, *Reading with Lincoln*, 200–209.
12. Garner, 30–34, 57–58.
13. Bray, *Reading with Lincoln*, 16–18; Garner, 74–78.
14. Whitney, *Life on the Circuit*, 177. Cf. Stevens, *Reporter's Lincoln*, 175.
15. Burlingame [online], 1:928–29.
16. Carpenter, *Six Months*, 273–74.
17. *HI*, 573 (Andrew H. Goodpasture; spelling corrected). Lincoln's text was Luke 17:37 and Matthew 24:28. Cf. Tarbell, "Humor in the White House," 20–21.
18. Thomas, *Abraham Lincoln*, 424–26.
19. Shelby M. Cullom, "Lincoln as I Knew Him," *Philadelphia Press*, February 7, 1904, scrapbook 15, p. 91, LCHL.
20. *ALLL*, 89.
21. Lincoln to Mrs. Orville H. Browning, April 1, 1838, *CW*, 1:117–18.
22. Whitney, "Abraham Lincoln," 468.
23. Horace Porter, speech, February 1889, scrapbook 15, p. 40, LCHL.

24. Brooks, "Personal Reminiscences," 563.
25. Whitney, "Abraham Lincoln," 468.
26. Brooks, "Personal Reminiscences," 564.
27. *HI*, 187 (Joseph Gillespie).
28. *HI*, 153.
29. *HI*, 641–42 (Thomas H. Nelson).
30. Burlingame, 1:301; cf. *RWAL*, 139.
31. Burlingame and Ettlinger, *Inside Lincoln's White House*, 132; Wilson, "Recollections," 516.
32. Carpenter, *Six Months*, 148–49.
33. *RWAL*, 453.
34. *RWAL*, 126.
35. *HI*, 85 (Samuel Haycraft).
36. Stevens, *Reporter's Lincoln*, 39–40.
37. Lincoln, "Remarks at Painesville, Ohio," February 16, 1861, *CW*, 4:218.
38. Brooks, "Personal Recollections," 228.
39. Conwell, *Why Lincoln Laughed*, 4.
40. Rourke, *American Humor*, 125–27.
41. Brooks, "Personal Reminiscences," 885.
42. *HI*, 396 (John B. Weber); *ALLL*, 50–51.
43. *RWAL*, 327.
44. Wilson, "Recollections," 516.
45. Brooks, "Personal Recollections," 228.
46. Brooks, "Personal Reminiscences," 565.
47. Stevens, *Reporter's Lincoln*, 91.
48. Brooks, "Personal Recollections," 228.
49. Garner, 360.
50. Burlingame [online], 1:959.
51. Burlingame and Ettlinger, *Inside Lincoln's White House*, 77.
52. Lamon, *Recollections*, 16–17.
53. *New York Herald*, February 19, 1864; *ALLL*, 22.
54. Wilson, "Recollections," 515.
55. Lincoln, "Bass-Ackwards," *CW*, 8:420; Hertz, *Hidden Lincoln*, 400.
56. Stevens, *Reporter's Lincoln*, 69.
57. Brooks, "Personal Reminiscences," 680.
58. Wilson, *Abraham Lincoln*, unpaginated.
59. Lincoln, "Speech in U.S. House of Representatives on the Presidential Question," July 27, 1848, *CW*, 1:509.
60. Lincoln, "First Debate with Stephen A. Douglas at Ottawa, Illinois," August 21, 1858, *CW*, 3:16; Lincoln, "Speech at Columbus, Ohio," September 16, 1859, *CW*, 3:402.

61. Hannibal Hamlin, "Lincoln," *Home Magazine*, February 1891; scrapbook 15, p. 71, LCHL.
62. Lincoln to Jesse W. Fell, Enclosing Autobiography, December 20, 1859, *CW*, 3:511–12.
63. Stevens, *Reporter's Lincoln*, 29.
64. Burlingame, 1:329.
65. *ALLL*, 66.
66. *RWAL*, 91–92.
67. Brooks, *Washington in Lincoln's Time*, 50–51.
68. *ALLL*, 80.
69. *Herndon's Lincoln*, 198–99.
70. Brooks, "Personal Recollections," 228; Wilson, "Recollections," 524.
71. Oberholtzer, *Jay Cooke*, 1:156.
72. Lamon, *Life of Lincoln*, 325; *HI*, 424 (J. D. Wickizer).
73. Grant, *Personal Memoirs*, 2:423.
74. Harris, "Recollections," scrapbook 45, p. 10, LCHL.
75. Weik, "Lincoln as a Lawyer," LCHL.
76. Williams, *Lincolnics*, 109.
77. Rice, 441–43.
78. Chambrun, "Personal Recollections," scrapbook 15, p. 132, LCHL.
79. Lamon, *Recollections*, 285.
80. McMinn, "Lincoln as Known to His Neighbors."
81. Field, *Memories*, 310.
82. Lincoln to George D. Ramsay, October 17, 1861, *CW*, 4:556. Cf. ibid., 5:109.
83. Raymond, *Life and Public Services*, 747–48.
84. Garner, 414.
85. Stevens, *Reporter's Lincoln*, 24–25, 103–4.
86. John M. Hay to Miles O'Reilly, November 22, 1863, John Hay Papers, Huntington Library.
87. Garner, 440, 535.
88. *HI*, 147.
89. Ibid., 69.
90. Ibid., 617, 644.
91. Garner, 202.
92. Burlingame, 1:54, 261.
93. Moses Hampton to Lincoln, March 30, 1849, ALP.
94. Moses Hampton to Lincoln, May 23, 1860, ALP.
95. Rice, 485–86.
96. *HI*, 443.
97. Burlingame, 1:55.

98. *HI*, 442 (Henry E. Dummer).
99. Lincoln, "Second Lecture on Discoveries and Inventions," [February 11, 1859], *CW*, 3:359–60.
100. *ALLL*, 64.
101. *HI*, 174 (Ellis), 438 (Christopher C. Brown).
102. Hertz, *Hidden Lincoln*, 398–99; Zall, *Abe Lincoln Laughing*, 100–101.
103. Carl Sandburg, interview with Joseph Fifer, Sandburg-Barrett Collection, Newberry Library, Chicago.
104. *ALLL*, 27–28.
105. *HI*, 128 (Nathaniel Grigsby).
106. Sandburg interview with Fifer.
107. *ALLL*, 79.
108. Sandburg interview with Fifer.
109. Thompson, *National Joker*, 1–8.
110. *Herndon's Lincoln*, 126.
111. Wilson, *Lincoln before Washington*, 55–73; Bray, "Power to Hurt," 44–51.
112. Burlingame, 1:140–41; Winger, *Lincoln, Religion, and Romantic Cultural Politics*, 15–18, 24, 44–45.
113. Whitney, *Lincoln the Citizen*, 47; Carpenter, *Six Months*, 51.
114. Schurz, *Reminiscences*, 2:93–94, 96.
115. Lincoln, "Fourth Debate with Stephen A. Douglas at Charleston, Illinois," September 18, 1858, *CW*, 3:146.
116. Lincoln, "Speech at Springfield, Illinois," July 17, 1858, *CW*, 2:520.
117. Rice, 2–4.
118. Weed, *Autobiography*, 612.
119. Carpenter, *Six Months*, 241.
120. *ALLL*, 77.
121. Rice, 30.
122. *ALLL*, 36.
123. Zall, *Abe Lincoln Laughing*, 88.
124. Rice, 510.
125. Brooks, "Personal Reminiscences," 564.
126. *ALLL*, 32–33.
127. *RWAL*, 9.
128. Ibid., 21.
129. *ALLL*, 77.
130. Neely, "Unbeknownst to Lincoln," 214.
131. *ALLL*, 66.
132. Burlingame, 1: 329.
133. *RWAL*, 482.
134. Carpenter, *Six Months*, 159.

135. Nicolay, *Personal Traits*, 284–85.
136. Carpenter, *Six Months*, 277.
137. Smith, "President Lincoln," 301; *ALLL*, 37–38.

3. A Just Laughter and the Moral Springs of Lincoln's Humor

1. *RWAL*, 457.
2. Garner, 449.
3. *Herndon's Lincoln*, 62n; *HI*, 69 (J. Rowan Herndon).
4. Nicolay, *Personal Traits of Abraham Lincoln*, 21–22.
5. Porter, *Campaigning with Grant*, 221–22.
6. *ALLL*, 92; Burlingame [online], 1:140–41.
7. McClure, *"Abe" Lincoln's Yarns and Stories*, 442–43.
8. *RWAL*, 502–3.
9. *ALLL*, 91.
10. *HI*, 172 (Abner Y. Ellis; spelling corrected; punctuation added).
11. Cole, *Memoirs*, 173.
12. Harrison, *Man Who Made Nasby*, 98.
13. Genesis 9:20–27, 16:1–10; Philemon, 1:8–21.
14. *Old Guard* 1 (1863), 9, 12, 38–39.
15. Ibid., 11; *New York Freeman's Journal*, April 25, 1863.
16. *Old Guard* 1 (1863), 40–43, 61; *New York Freeman's Journal*, May 2 and 16, 1863.
17. *Illinois State Register*, August 4, 1864; *Chicago Times*, August 4, 1864.
18. *Old Guard* 2 (1864), 140, 199–200, 224–25, 275.
19. Jones, introduction, xi–xiv.
20. *Philadelphia North American and United States Gazette*, November 12, 1864.
21. Locke, *Struggles of Nasby*, 13–14.
22. Harrison, *Man Who Made Nasby*, 14–15, 20, 23–24, 30–32, 85–86, 121; Jones, introduction, xi, xviii.
23. Harrison, *Man Who Made Nasby*, 86–87.
24. Locke, *Nasby Papers*, 12, 26, 33, 37–39.
25. Ibid., 1, 19, 27, 29–30.
26. Ibid., 3–4, 22–26, 41.
27. Ibid., 22.
28. Rice, 439–43, 446–47.
29. Ibid., 447–48; Welles, *Diary*, 585; Harris, *Lincoln's Last Months*, 56.
30. Thomas and Hyman, *Stanton*, 330. Cf. Burlingame and Ettlinger, *Inside Lincoln's White House*, 239.
31. Rice, 373.
32. Locke, *Struggles of Nasby*, 15. See, too, Harrison, *Man Who Made Nasby*, 112–13.

33. *Abraham Lincoln: An Exhibition*, 73; Harrison, *Man Who Made Nasby*, 115; *HI*, 167 (Swett).

34. Locke, *Nasby Papers*, 28, 33–34, 37–38.

35. Jones, introduction, xv.

36. Locke, *Nasby Papers*, 9, 34, 40.

37. Ibid., 35.

38. Rice, 442; Conwell, *Why Lincoln Laughed*, 135.

39. *HI*, 561.

40. Ibid., 166, 182–84, 350–51, 507. For similar reflections, see ibid., 4 (Horace White), 18–20 (William Graham Greene), 153 (Richard James Oglesby), 238 (Samuel C. Parks), 494 (George Eisenmeyer), 632 (Henry Clay Whitney). See also *Herndon's Lincoln*, 356–63.

41. Lincoln, "Fragment on Pro-slavery Theology," [October 1, 1858?], *CW*, 3:204–5.

42. Lincoln, "Story Written for Noah Brooks," [December 6, 1864], *CW*, 8:154–55.

43. Pryor, "Brief Encounter," 16–19, 22.

44. Rice, 446–47.

45. Lincoln, "Speech at Columbus, Ohio," September 16, 1859, *CW*, 3:400–425; Lincoln, "Notes for Speeches at Columbus and Cincinnati, Ohio," September 16, 17, 1859, *CW*, 3:425-36; Lincoln, "Speech at Cincinnati, Ohio," September 17, 1859, *CW*, 3:445–46; Lincoln, "Speech at Indianapolis, Indiana," September 19, 1859, *CW*, 3:470; Lincoln, "Speech at Leavenworth, Kansas," December 3, 1859, *CW*, 3:500.

46. Rice, 440, 447.

47. Harrison, *Man Who Made Nasby*, 112.

48. John McMahon to Lincoln, August 5, 1864; Lincoln to John McMahon, August 6, 1864; John G. Nicolay to John McMahon, August 6, 1864, ALP.

49. Burlingame, 2:809.

4. Purposes, Functions, Effects

1. Villard, *Memoirs*, 1:143.

2. *ALLL*, xii.

3. Brooks, "Personal Reminiscences," 675.

4. Harris, "Recollections of Abraham Lincoln," scrapbook 45, p. 10, LCHL.

5. *HI*, 499; Rice, 373.

6. Burlingame and Ettlinger, *Inside Lincoln's White House*, 194.

7. Chambrun, "Personal Recollections," scrapbook 15, p. 132, LCHL.

8. *RWAL*, 252. Cf. Carpenter, *Six Months*, 152.

9. Nicolay, *Personal Traits of Abraham Lincoln*, 16; *Herndon's Lincoln*, 355n; *RWAL*, 437–38; Browning and Gentry, *John M. Browning*, 12–13.

10. *RWAL*, 279. Cf. Ibid., 405.

11. Grinnell, *Men and Events*, 173–74.

12. *RWAL*, 241; Carpenter, *Six Months*, 150.

13. "High-Handed Outrage at Utica," in Browne, *Artemus Ward*, 34–35; *RWAL*, 416.

14. Welles, *Diary*, 216; Newell, *Orpheus C. Kerr Papers*; Rice, 448.

15. Brooks, "Personal Recollections," 229; Burlingame, *Lincoln Observed*, 218.

16. *RWAL*, 507.

17. Brooks, "Personal Reminiscences," 564.

18. Nicolay, "Lincoln's Literary Experiments," 825.

19. Burlingame [online], 1:1095.

20. McMinn, "Lincoln as Known to His Neighbors," scrapbook 15, p. 62, LCHL.

21. *ALLL*, xvii.

22. Stevens, *Reporter's Lincoln*, 61.

23. Edwards, "The Great Politician Who Was Afraid of Lincoln's Stories," scrapbook 5, p. 64, LCHL.

24. Burlingame [online], 2:2808.

25. Bray, "Power to Hurt," 51–53; Lincoln, "Speech in the Illinois Legislature concerning the State Bank," January 11, 1837, *CW*, 1:61–69.

26. Lincoln, "Speech at Kalamazoo, Michigan," August 27, 1856, *CW*, 2:362; Lincoln, "'A House Divided': Speech at Springfield, Illinois," June 16, 1858, *CW*, 2:467; Lincoln, "Speech at Springfield, Illinois," July 17, 1858, *CW*, 2:506; Lincoln, "First Debate with Stephen A. Douglas at Ottawa, Illinois," August 21, 1858, *CW*, 3:22.

27. Thomas, "Lincoln's Humor," 40.

28. Villard, *Memoirs*, 1:96.

29. Prokopowicz, *Did Lincoln Own Slaves?*, 39.

30. Garner, 195.

31. Burlingame, 1:930.

32. Burt, "Lincoln on His Own Story-Telling," 502.

33. John M. Hay to Miles O'Reilly, November 22, 1863, John Milton Hay Papers, Huntington Library.

34. Rice, 240.

35. Mitgang, *Abraham Lincoln*, 274.

36. *ALLL*, 28.

37. *Addresses Delivered at the Lincoln Dinner*, 307–8 (Theodore Burton).

38. Garner, 446–47.

39. Harris, "Recollections of Abraham Lincoln," scrapbook 45, p. 10, LCHL.

40. Rice, 428.

41. Burt, "Lincoln on His Own Story-Telling," 499–502.

42. Burlingame [online], 2:3811–12.

43. Burlingame [online], 1:928–29.

44. As told to Ida M. Tarbell by Albert J. Conant, undated memo, Tarbell Papers, Allegheny College. My thanks to Michael Burlingame.

45. Monaghan, *Diplomat in Carpet Slippers*, 187.

46. *RWAL*, 168.

47. Horace Porter, speech, February 1889, scrapbook 15, p. 40, LCHL.

48. Burlingame [online], 2:2391.

49. Neely, "Unbeknownst to Lincoln," 214.

50. Garner, 639.

51. Strong, *Diary*, 3:204–5.

52. *New York Times*, November 6, 1860.

53. *Vincennes Gazette*, December 22, 1860.

54. *Washington Reporter*, June 19, 1862; *San Francisco Evening Bulletin*, November 4, 1862.

55. John M. Hay to Miles O'Reilly, November 22, 1863, John M. Hay Papers, Huntington Library; Halpine, *Life and Adventures of O'Reilly*, 196.

56. Halpine, *Life and Adventures of O'Reilly*, 61.

57. *San Francisco Daily Evening Bulletin*, January 6, 1864; *Washington Reporter*, January 20, 1864.

58. *San Francisco Daily Evening Bulletin*, January 7, 1864.

59. *Liberator*, May 6, 1864.

60. Barnett, *Abraham Lincoln, the Peoples' Candidate*, 15–16.

61. *New York Evening Post*, February 17, 1864; *New York Herald*, February 19, 1864.

62. *Liberator*, December 9, 1864.

63. *Weekly Vincennes Western Sun*, May 26, 1860.

64. *New York Herald*, June 19, 1860.

65. Garner, 344.

66. Conant, "A Portrait Painter's Reminiscences," 514.

67. *New Haven Columbian Register*, January 12, 1861; *Baltimore Sun*, February 18, 1861.

68. McClintock, *Lincoln and the Decision for War*, 197.

69. Burlingame [online], 2:2120, 2172.

70. Wilson, *Lincoln in Caricature*, 140–41.

71. *Daily Constitutional* (Augusta, Ga.), June 2, 1861; *Daily Morning News* (Savannah, Ga.), February 17, 1862; *Dallas Weekly Herald*, July 5, 1862;

Richmond Examiner, December 5, 1862, November 11, 1863, July 13, August 22, 1864; *Macon Daily Telegraph,* January 2, March 18, 1863.

72. William Norwood (Georgetown) to unknown recipient, May 2, 1861, BR box 281(22), Huntington Library.

73. Burlingame [online], 1:1441; 2: 3262, 3618.

74. Pryor, "'Grand Old Duke of York,'" 9.

75. Burlingame [online], 2:3041.

76. Strong, *Diary,* 3:281–82.

77. Burlingame, 2:612.

78. Gordon, *Papers of Stanton and Anthony,* 1:514.

79. *Crisis,* September 3, 1862.

80. *Old Guard* 1 (February 1863), 47, (May 1863), 11.

81. *Wisconsin Daily Patriot,* January 2, 1863; *Weekly Vincennes Western Sun,* January 3, 1863.

82. Wilson, *Lincoln in Caricature,* 214–15.

83. *Weekly Patriot and Union* (Harrisburg), April 2, 1863.

84. *Illustrated New Age,* November 20, 1863.

85. *Cincinnati Daily Enquirer,* November 30, 1863.

86. Peatman, *Long Shadow,* 15.

87. *Weekly Vincennes Western Sun,* March 15, 1862.

88. *Old Guard* 1 (October–December 1863), 240.

89. *Wisconsin Daily Patriot,* September 25, 1863; *Weekly Patriot and Union* (Harrisburg), October 8, 1863.

90. *Weekly Patriot and Union* (Harrisburg), January 28, 1864.

91. *New York Herald,* September 20, 1863.

92. *New York Herald,* January 23, February 19, 20, 1864.

93. Pomeroy, *Next Presidential Election,* 4–8.

94. *Cincinnati Daily Enquirer,* February 10, 1864.

95. *Weekly Vincennes Western Sun,* April 9, 1864.

96. Lincoln, "Reply to Delegation from the National Union League," June 9, 1864, *CW,* 7:383–84.

97. *New Hampshire Patriot,* June 22, 1864.

98. Van Buren, *John Van Buren at Home,* 4–5.

99. Winthrop, *Great Speech . . . at New London,* 3–5.

100. Burlingame [online], 2:3765; *Newark Advocate,* August 5, 1864; *Weekly Vincennes Western Sun,* August 13, 20, 1864; *Cincinnati Daily Enquirer,* August 26, 1864.

101. *Liberator,* September 30, 1864; *Daily Ohio Statesman,* September 22, 1864.

102. *Cincinnati Daily Enquirer,* January 9, 1864.

103. *Mobile Daily Tribune,* March 26, 1864.

104. *Cincinnati Daily Enquirer,* June 20, 1864.

105. *Cincinnati Daily Enquirer*, July 12, 1864.

106. *Weekly Vincennes Western Sun*, July 30, 1864.

107. *Official Proceedings of the Democratic National Convention*, 50–51.

108. *Weekly Vincennes Western Sun*, September 10, 1864.

109. *World,* reprinted in *Cincinnati Daily Enquirer*, July 12, 1864.

110. *World,* September 9, 1864.

111. *Weekly Vincennes Western Sun*, April 9, 1864.

112. *Albany Argus*, reprinted in the *Liberator*, July 8, 1864.

113. *Cincinnati Daily Enquirer*, November 2, 1864.

114. *Democratic Presidential Campaign Songster*, 11.

115. McClellan, *Letter of Acceptance*, 3.

116. *Daily Ohio Statesman*, September 22, 1864.

117. D. M. Demarest to John M. Hay, August 2, 1864, ALP.

118. Lincoln, "Memorandum concerning Ward H. Lamon and the Antietam Episode," ca. September 12, 1864, *CW*, 7:548–49.

119. *RWAL*, 290.

120. A. J. Perkins to Ward Hill Lamon, September 10, 1864 (LN 2376); Ward Hill Lamon to A. J. Perkins, September 30, 1864 (LN 2378), Lamon Papers, Huntington Library.

121. Samuel Wilkeson to John G. Nicolay, September 21, 1864, ALP.

122. Lincoln, "Interview with Alexander W. Randall and Joseph T. Mills," August 19, 1864, *CW*, 7:506–7; Mills, *Loyal Road to Peace.*

123. *Stirring Appeals from Honored Veterans*, 94.

124. Coddington, *Crisis and the Man*, 7.

125. Barnett, *Abraham Lincoln, the Peoples' Candidate*, 2.

126. Wilson, *Lincoln in Caricature*, 284–85.

127. *Harper's Weekly*, September 17, 1864 (Wilson plate 140).

Epilogue

1. *Vincennes Weekly Western Sun*, June 9, 1866, from the *La Crosse Democrat.*

2. Newell, *Martyr President*, 20.

3. Chesebrough, *No Sorrow Like Our Sorrow*, 24–25.

4. *ALLL*, 41–85.

5. Schwartz, *Abraham Lincoln and the Forge of National Memory*, 107–42, 167–70.

6. *HI*, 174.

7. Villard, *Memoirs*, 1: 93–94, 143–44.

BIBLIOGRAPHY

Manuscript Sources

John Milton Hay Papers, Huntington Library, San Marino, California
Ward Hill Lamon Papers, Huntington Library, San Marino, California
Abraham Lincoln Collection, Huntington Library, San Marino, California
Abraham Lincoln Papers, Library of Congress
Sandburg-Barrett Collection, Newberry Library, Chicago
Ida M. Tarbell Collection of Lincolniana, Allegheny College, Meadville,
  Pennsylvania

Newspapers

Baltimore Sun
Chicago Times
Cincinnati Daily Enquirer
Columbian Register (New Haven, Conn.)
The Crisis (Columbus, Ohio)
Daily Constitutional (Augusta, Ga.)
Daily Morning News (Savannah, Ga.)
Dallas Weekly Herald
Harper's Weekly (New York)
Illinois State Register (Springfield)
The Liberator (Boston)
Mobile Daily Tribune
Newark Advocate
New Hampshire Patriot (Concord)
New York Evening Post
New York Freeman's Journal
New York Herald
New York Times
Ohio Statesman (Columbus)
Philadelphia North American and United States Gazette
Richmond Examiner
Salem (Mass.) Register
San Francisco Evening Bulletin
Vincennes (Ind.) Gazette
Vincennes (Ind.) Western Sun
Washington (D.C.) Reporter
Weekly Patriot and Union (Harrisburg, Pa.)
Wisconsin Daily Patriot (Madison)
The World (New York)

Books, Pamphlets, Essays, Articles, Theses

Abraham Lincoln: An Exhibition at the Library of Congress in Honor of the 150th Anniversary of His Birth. Washington, D.C.: Library of Congress and Lincoln Sesquicentennial Commission, 1959.

Adderup, Andrew. *Lincolniana, or The Humors of Uncle Abe: Second Joe Miller.* New York: J. F. Feeks, 1864.

Addresses Delivered at the Lincoln Dinner of the Republican Club of New York . . . 1887–1909. New York: Republican Club of New York, 1909.

Arnold, Isaac N. *The Life of Abraham Lincoln.* Chicago: Jansen, McClurg, 1884.

Baldwin, Joseph G. *The Flush Times of Alabama and Mississippi: A Series of Sketches.* New York: D. Appleton and Company, 1854.

Barnett, T. J. *Abraham Lincoln, the Peoples' Candidate: Speech . . . in Richmond, Indiana, October 6, 1864.* N.p.: Union State Central Committee, 1864.

Boritt, Gabor S., ed. *The Historian's Lincoln: Pseudohistory, Psychohistory, and History.* Urbana: University of Illinois Press, 1984.

Bray, Robert. "'The Power to Hurt': Lincoln's Early Use of Satire and Invective." *Journal of the Abraham Lincoln Association* 16, no.1 (Winter 1995): 39–58.

Bray, Robert C. *Reading with Lincoln.* Carbondale: Southern Illinois University Press, 2010.

Bridges, Roger W., ed. "Three Letters from a Lincoln Law Student." *Journal of the Illinois State Historical Society* 66, no.1 (Spring 1973): 79–87.

Brooks, Noah. "Personal Recollections of Lincoln." *Harper's New Monthly Magazine,* July 1865, 222–30.

———. "Personal Reminiscences of Lincoln." *Scribner's Monthly* 15, no.4–5 (February and March 1878).

———. *Washington in Lincoln's Time.* New York: Century, 1895.

Browne, Francis Fisher. *The Every-Day Life of Abraham Lincoln.* New York: N. D. Thompson, 1886.

[Browne, Charles F.] *Artemus Ward: His Book.* New York: Carleton, 1862.

Browning, John, and Curt Gentry. *John M. Browning: American Gunmaker.* New York: Doubleday, 1964.

Bunker, Gary L. *From Rail-Splitter to Icon: Lincoln's Image in Illustrated Periodicals, 1860–1865.* Kent, Ohio: Kent State University Press, 2001.

Burlingame, Michael. *Abraham Lincoln: A Life.* 2 vols. Baltimore: Johns Hopkins University Press, 2008.

———. *Abraham Lincoln: A Life,* the Unedited Manuscript. Lincoln Studies Center, Knox College, Galesburg, Ill. https://www.knox.edu/about-knox/lincoln-studies-center/burlingame-abraham-lincoln-a-life.

———, ed. *Lincoln Observed: Civil War Dispatches of Noah Brooks.* Baltimore: Johns Hopkins University Press, 1998.

———, ed. *An Oral History of Abraham Lincoln: John G. Nicolay's Interviews and Essays.* Carbondale: Southern Illinois University Press, 1996.

Burlingame, Michael, and John R. Turner Ettlinger, eds. *Inside Lincoln's White House: The Complete Civil War Diaries of John Hay.* Carbondale: Southern Illinois University Press, 1997.

Burt, Silas W. "Lincoln on His Own Story-Telling." *Century Magazine* 73, no.4 (February 1907).

Busey, Samuel C. *Personal Reminiscences and Recollections . . .* Washington, D.C.: Dornan, 1895.

Carpenter, Francis B. *Six Months at the White House with Abraham Lincoln.* New York: Hurd and Houghton, 1866.

Chambrun, Marquis de. "Personal Recollections of Mr. Lincoln." *Scribner's Magazine,* January 1893. Scrapbook 15, p. 132, Lincoln Collection, Huntington Library.

Chesebrough, David B. *No Sorrow Like Our Sorrow: Northern Protestant Ministers and the Assassination of Lincoln.* Kent, Ohio: Kent State University Press, 1994.

Chrisman, Herring. *Memoirs of Lincoln.* Mapleton, Iowa: W. H. Chrisman, 1930.

Coddington, David S. *The Crisis and the Man: Address . . . Nov. 1, 1864.* New York: William Oland Bourne, 1865.

Cole, Cornelius. *Memoirs of Cornelius Cole: Ex-Senator of the U.S. from California.* New York: McLoughlin Brothers, 1908.

Conant, Alban Jasper. "A Portrait Painter's Reminiscences of Lincoln." *McClure's Magazine* 32, no. 5 (March 1909).

Conway, Moncure D. *Autobiography: Memories and Experiences.* 2 vols. Boston: Houghton Mifflin, 1904.

Conwell, Russell H. *Why Lincoln Laughed.* New York: Harper and Brothers, 1922.

Democratic Presidential Campaign Songster: No. 1. McClellan and Pendleton . . . New York: J. F. Feeks, 1864.

Derby, George H. *Phoenixiana, or Sketches and Burlesques.* New York: D. Appleton and Company, 1856.

Donald, David Herbert. *Lincoln.* New York: Simon and Schuster, 1995.

Edwards, E. J. "The Great Politician Who Was Afraid of Lincoln's Stories." Scrapbook 5, p. 64, Lincoln Collection, Huntington Library.

Evans, Robert. "The Humour of History and the History of Humour." *Oxford Historian* 9 (2011): 44–58.

Faust, Drew Gilpin. *This Republic of Suffering: Death and the American Civil War.* New York: Alfred A. Knopf, 2008.

Fehrenbacher, Don E., and Virginia Fehrenbacher, comps. and eds. *Recollected Words of Abraham Lincoln*. Stanford, Calif.: Stanford University Press, 1996.

Field, Maunsell B. *Memories of Many Men and of Some Women*. New York: Harper and Brothers, 1874.

Garner, Wayne Lee. "Abraham Lincoln and the Uses of Humor." PhD dissertation, University of Iowa, 1963.

Gordon, Ann D., ed. *The Selected Papers of Elizabeth Cady Stanton and Susan B. Anthony*. 4 vols. New Brunswick, N.J.: Rutgers University Press, 1997–2006.

Grant, U. S. *Personal Memoirs of U. S. Grant*. 2 vols. New York: 1885–86.

Grinnell, Josiah Bushnell. *Men and Events of Forty Years: Autobiographical Reminiscences . . .* Boston: D. Lothrop, 1891.

Guelzo, Allen C. *Abraham Lincoln: Redeemer President*. Grand Rapids, Mich.: W. B. Eerdmans, 1999.

Halpine, Charles G. *The Life and Adventures, Songs, Services, and Speeches of Private Miles O'Reilly (47th Regiment, New York Volunteers)*. New York: Carleton, 1864.

Harris, Gibson William. "Recollections of Abraham Lincoln." *Women's Home Companion*, November 1903, 9–11; December 1903, 14–15; January 1904, 13–15; February 1904, 10–11, 24. Scrapbook 45, pp. 9–12, Lincoln Collection, Huntington Library.

Harris, William C. *Lincoln's Last Months*. Cambridge, Mass.: Belknap Press, 2004.

Harrison, John M. *The Man Who Made Nasby, David Ross Locke*. Chapel Hill: University of North Carolina Press, 1969.

Herndon, William H., and Jesse Weik. *Herndon's Lincoln*. Edited by Douglas L. Wilson and Rodney O. Davis. Urbana: University of Illinois Press, 2006.

Hertz, E. *The Hidden Lincoln from the Letters and Papers of William H. Herndon*. New York: Viking Press, 1938.

Hill, Frederick Trevor. "Lincoln the Lawyer." *Century Magazine* 71, no.6 (April 1906): 939–53.

———. "The Lincoln-Douglas Debates Fifty Years After." *Century Magazine* 77, no.1 (November 1908): 3–19.

Holland, J. G. *Life of Abraham Lincoln*. Springfield, Mass.: G. Bill, 1866.

Holzer, Harold. *Lincoln and the Power of the Press: The War for Public Opinion*. New York: Simon and Schuster, 2014.

Joe Miller's Jests, or The Wits Vade Mecum. London, 1739. U.S. edition: Philadelphia, 1817.

Johannsen, Robert W. *Stephen A. Douglas*. New York: Oxford University Press, 1973.

Jones, Joseph. Introduction to *The Struggles of Petroleum V. Nasby*, by David Ross Locke. Boston: Beacon Press, 1963.

Kaplan, Fred. *Lincoln: The Biography of a Writer*. New York: Harper, 2008.

Kent, Christopher. "War Cartooned/Cartoon War: Matt Morgan and the American Civil War in *Fun* and *Frank Leslie's Illustrated Newspaper*." *Victorian Periodicals Review* 36 no. 2 (Summer 2003): 158–81.

Lamon, Ward Hill. *Life of Abraham Lincoln* . . . Boston: J. R. Osgood, 1872.

———. *Recollections of Abraham Lincoln, 1847–1865*. Edited by Dorothy Lamon Teillard. Washington, D.C.: Cambridge University Press, 1911.

Lincoln, Abraham. *The Collected Works of Abraham Lincoln*. Edited by Roy P. Basler. 9 vols. New Brunswick, N.J.: Rutgers University Press, 1953–55.

Locke, David Ross. *The Nasby Papers: Letters and Sermons Containing the Views on the Topics of the Day, of Petroleum V. Nasby, "Paster uv the Church of the Noo Dispensashun."* Indianapolis: C. O. Perrine, 1864.

———. *The Struggles (Social, Financial, and Political) of Petroleum V. Nasby, . . . With an Introduction by Hon. Charles Sumner.* Boston: I. N. Richardson, 1872.

McBride, Robert W. *Personal Recollections of Abraham Lincoln*. Indianapolis: Bobbs-Merrill, 1926.

McClellan, George B. *The Democratic Platform: General McClellan's Letter of Acceptance.* [New York, 1864.]

McClintock, Russell. *Lincoln and the Decision for War: The Northern Response to Secession.* Chapel Hill: University of North Carolina Press, 2008.

McClure, Alexander K. *"Abe" Lincoln's Yarns and Stories* . . . Philadelphia: Elliott, 1901.

McCulloch, Hugh. *Men and Measures of Half of a Century: Sketches and Comments.* New York: C. Scribner's Sons, 1888.

McMinn, P. K. "Lincoln as Known to His Neighbors." *Saturday Evening Post*, February 13, 1904. Scrapbook 15, p. 62, Lincoln Collection, Huntington Library.

Mills, John T. *The Loyal Road to Peace and the Disloyal Road to Ruin: President Lincoln on Democratic Strategy.* [N.p.: 1864.]

Mitgang, Herbert, ed. *Abraham Lincoln: A Press Portrait.* Chicago: Quadrangle Books, 1971.

Monaghan, Jay. *Diplomat in Carpet Slippers: Abraham Lincoln Deals with Foreign Affairs.* Indianapolis: Bobbs-Merrill, 1945.

Neely, Mark E. *The Boundaries of American Political Culture in the Civil War Era.* Chapel Hill: University of North Carolina Press, 2005.

———. "'Unbeknownst to Lincoln': A Note on Radical Pacification in Missouri during the Civil War." *Civil War History* 44, no.3 (September 1998): 212–16.

Newell, R. H. *The Orpheus C. Kerr Papers.* 3 vols. New York: Blakeman and Mason, 1862–65.

———. *The Martyr President.* New York: Carleton, 1865.

Nicolay, Helen. *Personal Traits of Abraham Lincoln.* New York: Century, 1912.

Nicolay, John G. "Lincoln's Literary Experiments." *Century Magazine* 47 (1894).

Oberholtzer, Ellis Paxson. *Jay Cooke: Financier of the Civil War.* 2 vols. Philadelphia: G. W. Jacobs, 1907.

Official Proceedings of the Democratic National Convention. Chicago: Times Steam Book and Job Printing House, 1864.

Old Abe's Joker, or Wit at the White House. New York: R. M. De Witt, 1863.

Old Abe's Jokes, Fresh from Abraham's Bosom. New York: T. R. Dawley, 1864.

The Old Guard. New York: C. Chauncey Burr, 1863–70.

Only Authentic Life of Abraham Lincoln, Alias "Old Abe": . . . also of Gen. George B. McClellan, Alias "Little Mac." New York: J. C. Haney, 1864.

Onstot, Thompson Gains. *Pioneers of Menard and Mason Counties. . . .* Forest City, Ill.: T. G. Onstot, 1902.

Peatman, Jared. *The Long Shadow of Lincoln's Gettysburg Address.* Carbondale: Southern Illinois University Press, 2013.

Peterson, Merrill D. *Lincoln in American Memory.* New York: Oxford University Press, 1994.

Pomeroy, S. C. *The Next Presidential Election.* [Washington, D.C.: 1864.]

Porter, Horace. *Campaigning with Grant.* New York: Century, 1897.

Prokopowicz, Gerald J. *Did Lincoln Own Slaves? And Other Frequently Asked Questions about Abraham Lincoln.* New York: Pantheon Books, 2008.

Pryor, Elizabeth Brown. "Brief Encounter: A New York Cavalryman's Striking Conversation with Abraham Lincoln." *Journal of the Abraham Lincoln Association* 30, no. 2 (Summer 2009): 1–24.

———. "'The Grand Old Duke of York': How Abraham Lincoln Lost the Confidence of His Military Command." Author's collection.

Quin's Jests, or The Facetious Man's Pocket Companion. London: S. Bladon, 1766.

Randall, James G. *Lincoln the President: Midstream.* New York: Dodd, Mead, 1952.

Raymond, Henry J. *The Life and Public Services of Abraham Lincoln.* New York: Derby and Miller, 1865.

Remsburg, John E. *Abraham Lincoln: Was He a Christian?* New York: Truth Seeker, 1893.

Rice, Allen Thorndike, ed. *Reminiscences of Abraham Lincoln by Distinguished Men of His Time.* New York: North American Publishing, 1886.

Rourke, Constance. *American Humor: A Study of the National Character.* Garden City, N.Y.: Doubleday, 1953.

Schurz, Carl. *Reminiscences of Carl Schurz.* 3 vols. New York: McClure, 1907–8.

Schwartz, Barry. *Abraham Lincoln and the Forge of National Memory.* Chicago: University of Chicago Press, 2000.

Shenk, Joshua Wolf. *Lincoln's Melancholy: How Depression Challenged a President and Fuelled His Greatness.* Boston: Houghton Mifflin, 2005.

Sloane, Arthur A. *Humor in the White House: The Wit of Five American Presidents.* Jefferson, N.C.: McFarland, 2001.

Smith, Goldwin. "President Lincoln." *Macmillan's Magazine* 11, no. 64 (February 1865): 300–305.

Speed, Joshua F. *Reminiscences of Abraham Lincoln . . .* Louisville: J. P. Morton, 1884.

Stevens, Walter B. *A Reporter's Lincoln.* Edited by Michael Burlingame. Lincoln: University of Nebraska Press, 1998.

Stewart, James Brewer. *Wendell Phillips: Liberty's Hero.* Baton Rouge: Louisiana State University Press, 1986.

Stirring Appeals from Honored Veterans: Democratic Statesmen and Generals to the Loyal Sons of the Union. . . . Albany, N.Y.: Weed, Parsons, 1864.

Stoddard, William O. *Inside the White House in War Times.* New York: C. L. Webster, 1890.

Stott, Richard Biggs. *Jolly Fellows: Male Milieus in Nineteenth-Century America.* Baltimore: Johns Hopkins University Press, 2009.

Strong, George Templeton. *Diary of George Templeton Strong.* Edited by Allan Nevins and Milton Halsey Thomas. 4 vols. New York: Macmillan, 1952.

Tarbell, Ida M. *The Life of Abraham Lincoln.* 4 vols. New York: Lincoln Historical Society, 1924.

Thomas, Benjamin Platt. "Lincoln's Humor: An Analysis." *Papers of the Abraham Lincoln Association* 3 (1981), 28–47.

———. *Abraham Lincoln: A Biography.* New York: Knopf, 1952.

Thomas, Benjamin P., and Harold Hyman. *Stanton: The Life and Times of Lincoln's Secretary of War.* New York: Knopf, 1962.

Thompson, Todd Nathan. *The National Joker: Abraham Lincoln and the Politics of Satire.* Carbondale: Southern Illinois University Press, 2015.

Uncle Abe's Comic Almanac. Philadelphia: Fisher, 1865.

Van Buren, John. *John Van Buren at Home. His Great Speech at Hudson, Oct. 27, 1864.* [New York: 1864.]

Villard, Henry. *Memoirs of Henry Villard: Journalist and Financier, 1835–1900.* 2 vols. Boston: Houghton Mifflin, 1904.

Wagenknecht, *Edward. Abraham Lincoln: His Life, Work, and Character; An Anthology.* New York: Creative Age Press, 1947.

Weed, Thurlow, *Autobiography.* Edited by Harriet A. Weed. Boston: Houghton Mifflin, 1884.

Weik, Jesse W. "Lincoln as a Lawyer." *Century Magazine*, June 1904. Scrapbook 15, p. 150, Lincoln Collection, Huntington Library.

Welles, Gideon. *The Civil War Diary of Gideon Welles, Lincoln's Secretary of the Navy: The Original Manuscript Edition.* Edited by William E. Gienapp and Erica L. Gienapp. Galesburg, Ill.: Knox College Lincoln Studies Center; Urbana: University of Illinois Press, 2014.

Whitney, Henry C. "Abraham Lincoln: A Study from Life." *Arena* 19 (April 1898).

———. *Life on the Circuit with Lincoln.* Boston: Estes, 1892.

———. *Lincoln the Citizen.* New York: Current Literature, 1907.

Williams, Henry Llewellyn. *Lincolnics: Familiar Sayings of Abraham Lincoln.* New York: Putnam, 1906.

Wilson, Douglas L. *Honor's Voice: The Transformation of Abraham Lincoln.* New York: Knopf, 1998.

———. *Lincoln before Washington: New Perspectives on the Illinois Years.* Urbana: University of Illinois Press, 1997.

Wilson, Douglas L., Rodney O. Davis, and Terry Wilson, eds. *Herndon's Informants: Letters, Interviews, and Statements about Abraham Lincoln.* Urbana: University of Illinois Press, 1998.

Wilson, James Grant. "Recollections of Lincoln," *Putnam's Magazine* 5, no. 6 (March 1909): 670–81.

Wilson, Rufus Rockwell. *Lincoln in Caricature: A Historical Collection . . .* New York: Horizon Press, 1953.

Wilson, William Bender. *Abraham Lincoln as I Knew Him: An Address.* [Andalusia, Pa.?,] 1909.

Winger, Stewart. *Lincoln, Religion, and Romantic Cultural Politics.* DeKalb: Northern Illinois University Press, 2003.

Winthrop, Robert C. *Great Speech . . . at New London, Conn., October 18 . . .* [New York: 1864.]

Zall, P. M., ed. *Abe Lincoln Laughing: Humorous Anecdotes from Original Sources by and about Abraham Lincoln.* Berkeley: University of California Press, 1982.

Zall, Paul M., ed. *Abe Lincoln's Legacy of Laughter: Humorous Stories by and about Abraham Lincoln.* Knoxville: University of Tennessee Press, 2007.

INDEX

Page numbers in italics indicate figures.

Richard Carwardine is a Distinguished Fellow of the Rothermere American Institute at the University of Oxford, where he previously served as Rhodes Professor of American History and as president of Corpus Christi College. His analytical biography *Lincoln* won the Lincoln Prize in 2004. His other work includes *Transatlantic Revivalism: Popular Evangelicalism in Britain and America, 1790–1865*; *Evangelicals and Politics in Antebellum America*; and (with Jay Sexton) *The Global Lincoln*.

CONCISE
LINCOLN
LIBRARY

This series of concise books fills a need for short studies of the life, times, and legacy of President Abraham Lincoln. Each book gives readers the opportunity to quickly achieve basic knowledge of a Lincoln-related topic. These books bring fresh perspectives to well-known topics, investigate previously overlooked subjects, and explore in greater depth topics that have not yet received book-length treatment. For a complete list of current and forthcoming titles, see www.conciselincolnlibrary.com.

Other Books in the Concise Lincoln Library